P9-DES-399

THE STORY OF STEWARDSHIP

In the United States of America

THE STORY
OF STEWARDSHIP

In the United States of America

By

GEORGE A. E. SALSTRAND, TH.D.

Professor of New Testament Interpretation
and Evangelism
Tennessee Temple Schools
Chattanooga, Tennessee

BAKER BOOK HOUSE
Grand Rapids 6, Michigan
1956

PRINTED IN THE UNITED STATES OF AMERICA

FOREWORD

A careful and thoughtful student of stewardship for many years, Dr. George A. E. Salstrand has produced a thrilling and informing story of stewardship in the United States. His treatment is comprehensive, detailed and fair.

Not only does he deal with the rise and progress of stewardship within the major Protestant denominations of America but within the smaller ones too. He thoughtfully weighs men, movements, principles and statistical reports having to do with stewardship. Here the reader will learn the history of tithing in our country, and the meaning of such projects as the Lord's acre plan, the Lord's hour, and the Belmont plan. The work of noted stewardship promoters, such as Thomas Kane, Henry Lansdell and Ralph S. Cushman receives due consideration.

If American Christianity, in this period of unprecedent material prosperity, responds to its opportunity to evangelize the world, it will have to travel further and faster down the road of Biblical stewardship. This book shows how far we have come, and creates incentive to go the rest of the way.

Chicago, Illinois   Faris D. Whitesell

27874

ACKNOWLEDGMENT

This exhaustive study could hardly have been completed without the help received from numerous sources. The author desires to acknowledge his indebtedness to: Dr. Peder Stianson, Dean of the Northern Baptist Seminary and head of the Department of Church History, whose class lectures inspired this additional research; Dr. Farris D. Whitesell, professor of Evangelism and Ecclesiology of the Northern Baptist Seminary, for many helpful suggestions; Dr. James W. Workman, until recently Associate Secretary of the General Board of Lay Activities of the Methodist Church, for making available much general and denominational stewardship material; Dr. Harry S. Myers, for thirty years Secretary of the United Stewardship Council of the Churches of Christ in America, who made available helpful material including statistics of the Council covering a twenty-one year period; Dr. Earle V. Pierce, who furnished a large quantity of stewardship tracts collected over a period of years; Dr. John E. Simpson, pastor of the First United Presbyterian Church of Oak Park, Illinois, author of several books on stewardship, who provided helpful counsel and made available his stewardship library; A. H. Johnson of the Layman Foundation, who supplied historical data and material published by the Layman Tithing Foundation; Lawrence Bjorndahl, certified accountant, whose staff calculated the per capita giving for various causes during certain years in the several denominations; and the Rev. T. K. Thompson, Executive Secretary of the Joint Department of Stewardship and Benevolence who furnished helpful material including the *Statistics of Giving* for the past fifteen years as well as recent issues of *Stewardship Facts,* a yearly publication; and to the noble company of men who in the different denominations are charged with the responsibilities of stewardship promotion, and who took time to write letters describing the situation in their respective denominations.

G.A.E.S.

PREFACE

One summer Sunday afternoon a country lad of seventeen, who had recently become a Christian, read an article in a religious periodical on the subject of the tithe.

It contained the story of William Colgate who as a poor lad began to tithe his meager income. Blessings resulted and as time went on he set aside increasingly larger proportions of his growing income for Christian causes, until he became one of the great benefactors of mankind through the Scriptural use of his money.

The young man who read this account resolved that he too would tithe his income. The practice of tithing plus frequent additional offerings has resulted in many blessings through the years. The lad of the story is the author of this book.

Later, as a pastor, it became his privilege to preach the great principles of stewardship with special emphasis on the tithe. Now as a teacher in an institution of higher learning, the author continues to experience heartfelt satisfaction in the course of the regular studies to pass on to his students from time to time the fundamentals of stewardship.

In order that truths concerning the tithe might be more clearly set forth so that a larger number could be reached, a booklet was written by the author entitled, *The Tithe, The Minimum Standard for Christian Giving.* The treatise, now in its second printing, is available from the publishers of this new and larger volume.

Research on the subject of the tithe indicated that this biblical doctrine was only recently rediscovered by American Christians and the revival of stewardship is largely an American contribution to theological thinking. Yet no history of this important subject was in existence.

That someone should assemble a history became apparent. Thus the research for this volume had its genesis. The whole realm of stewardship as developed in American thinking was investigated. Over one hundred books on the subject were gathered. Church histories were gleaned for information and magazine articles perused. Contact was made with nearly every denominational and interdenominational stewardship agency in existence. Specific questions were submitted. Approximately four hundred tracts and pamphlets were assembled and many vital stewardship facts were garnered.

Finally the completed manuscript was ready for publication. It was the year 1943 and World War II was at the height of its fury. Publication costs had skyrocketed. Paper was rationed. During such a time no publisher could afford to take risks on an unknown author's work. The manuscript was laid aside.

Eleven years passed in which significant stewardship history was made. It was a period characterized by mounting interest and increased emphasis regarding the tithe. The need for making the inspiring story of American stewardship development known to the Christian public became even more apparent. It was under these circumstances that representatives of the Baker Book House extended to the author the invitation to bring the manuscript up to date for publication.

More research was necessary because great quantities of new literature had been published relating to the subject. Though the list is not complete, the bibliography lists fifty-two additional books written since the war. Contact was made with the new group of stewardship leaders who assumed office during the interval. Two hundred additional tracts were added to the original collection making a total of six hundred.

Thus at last the stewardship story was ready for the Christian public. This is the first known attempt to reduce the history of the stewardship movement to writing. Completeness is not claimed. Contact was limited to the denominations with stewardship officials insofar as they could be located. Not every official responded, and not all of the reports obtained have been recorded.

As this volume is sent forth, it is the author's hope that the reader may find benefit. Instructors in Christian schools will welcome a history of stewardship. Ministers will find in this book a source of historical and illustrative stewardship preaching material. Sunday School teachers will discover that this book provides valuable supplementary material for lessons with a stewardship emphasis. To every layman this book should bring inspiration. And may all who read truly become "good stewards of the manifold grace of God."

George A. E. Salstrand

Chattanooga, Tennessee

CONTENTS

LIST OF FIGURES

INTRODUCTION

The purpose of this treatise is to trace the record of stewardship from colonial times to our present day, seeking to determine insofar as possible the origin, growth, and development of the stewardship movement.

Since stewardship promotion is largely an American contribution to theological thought, it is important to know something of its history. Like many other movements it is best understood in the light of history. Many a stewardship statement becomes more meaningful when viewed in relation to its historical background.

Stewardship in its fullest sense has to do with all the relationships of life, but in this study is concerned primarily with finances.

The first part deals with the general development of stewardship as a movement within the religious life of the nation. The second part deals with the specific development of stewardship within the various denominations.

The value of such a comprehensive study as this is apparent when the scarcity of integrated information in this field is realized. Although historical snatches are available, no connected history of American stewardship has previously been attempted.

In 1906 Henry Lansdell, an Anglican clergyman and professor, of Blackheath, England, issued his monumental work on the tithe in two volumes entitled, *The Sacred Tenth*. He traced the history of the tithe from antiquity to his day. Volume Two deals briefly with tithing in America. Nothing is said about the broader term, stewardship.

In 1913, A. L. Vail, a Baptist minister, produced a small volume entitled *Stewardship Among Baptists*. The first half of this little volume presents numerous, long, and tedious quotations from old Baptist records dealing with such subjects as ministerial support, giving, tithing, and stewardship. Although tedious, it is valuable because of the historical data concerning stewardship among Baptists.

In 1914, Harvey Reeves Calkins, a Methodist missionary, wrote one of the most significant books of his generation on the subject of stewardship entitled, *A Man and His Money*, which contained a brief historical sketch of the origin and growth of the stewardship movement.

In 1922, James W. Hensey, a Methodist clergyman, wrote *Storehouse Tithing,* or *Stewardship Up-To-Date.* This volume is valuable from the historical standpoint because it tells the story of the origin of the Storehouse Tithing Movement and a few details concerning its success in New York state.

In 1938 Dr. H. C. Weber, then Director of the Every Member Canvass Promotion of the Presbyterian Chuch, U.S.A., and president of the United Stewardship Council, wrote *The Horizons of Stewardship* in which a short chapter is devoted to outlining the historical background of stewardship in America.

In 1939 Dr. William Warren Sweet wrote *The Story of Religion in America.* A chapter on *The Era Of Organization* gives a splendid view of the rise of Modern Missions and other benevolent enterprises in America.

Also in 1939 John R. Mott wrote *Five Decades and a Forward View.* Chapters entitled *The Student Missionary Uprising* and *The Laymen's Missionary Movement* are very helpful in that they relate the history both of the Student Volunteer Movement and the Laymen's Missionary Movement, which two organizations exerted a helpful influence in the history of stewardship.

Other sources of data for this study include American denominational histories, numerous pieces of American stewardship literature, personal letters from at least forty denominational and interdenominational stewardship officials, tracts and pamphlets from nearly twenty-five denominations whose officials answered inquiries, the yearbooks of the denominations, and stewardship articles appearing in various religious periodicals.

Chapter I

MINISTERIAL SUPPORT IN YOUNG AMERICA

STEWARDSHIP has been spoken of as an American contribution to theological thinking, which is largely true. Liberty in the new world released the American pioneers from the shackles of the old world and its binding customs.

In the old world the most common means of support for the churches was subsidy by the state, supplemented by fees for such church ministrations as baptisms, marriages, funerals, etc.

This procedure was imported by some of the colonists, but soon abandoned. Following formation of the Union and adoption of the Constitution, separation of church and state became an American principle, creating the necessity for finding other means of supporting the churches.

In the literature of the colonial period, the term "stewardship" seems to have no place. During that period there was no widespread missionary program that challenged people to give. In this chapter we will note some of the ways in which various churches of the period handled the problem of supporting their pastors.

I. THE EPISCOPALIANS

The first English colonists who came to America represented the Church of England, known also as the Established Church, and settled in Jamestown, Virginia. Among the first one hundred and five colonists, who immigrated here in 1607, was Robert Hunt, a chaplain, described as a man "of preserving fortitude and modest worth." This clergyman, and others who followed, presented the problem of ministerial support.

As the colony grew, each parish was made responsible for maintaining its own minister. After 1662 the ministers were to receive a uniform salary, namely 16,000 pounds of tobacco. This rule worked a hardship on many of the Virginia clergymen since the price of tobacco was on a downward trend. Discontent also resulted from the fact that plant varieties differed in value. In certain counties, where a better grade tobacco was normally raised, the ministers often received double the value of the same amount of poor grade tobacco received by ministers serving other districts. Needless to say, this method was unsatisfactory for consistent ministerial support.

II. The Congregationalists

The Congregational Church traces its beginning to the Puritan Colonies. The first such colony was established at Plymouth by the Mayflower Pilgrims who in 1620 landed on the New England shores.

More influential were the settlements about Massachusetts Bay. One historian described this colony as "superior in wealth, station and capacity."

In the year 1628 the first Puritans arrived at the place now called Salem. By 1640 some twenty thousand had found their way across the Atlantic to the Massachusetts Bay Colony.

By the middle of the seventeenth century four Puritan colonies were firmly rooted in New England soil, and the Congregational Church was the dominating influence. It was a period of rapid development in American Congregationalism. Some of the noted expositors of the Congregational system of church government were John Cotton of Boston, Richard Mather of Dorchester, John Davenport of New Haven and Thomas Hooker of Connecticut.

The Reverend John Cotton, one of the most outstanding of the early Congregational leaders, recorded his views on giving in his journal. It reveals that on May 2, 1639, he preached from II Kings 8:8 which reads: "Take a present in thine hand, and go to meet the man of God." In this message he declared that when magistrates are forced to provide for the maintenance of ministers, then the churches are in a state of decline. He advocated that the minister's support be raised by voluntary contributions, not by taxation, which he said had always been accompanied with pride, contention, and sloth.

Joseph S. Clark, the Congregational Church historian, pointed out that their ministerial support was managed with great simplicity. The deacons were expected to gather up the free gifts of the congregation and deliver them to the minister if the regular offerings proved insufficient.

The custom of the Boston church about the year 1640 is described in volume two of the *Massachusetts Historical Collection*. Following the regular afternoon worship service, before the assembly dispersed, one of the deacons exhorted: "Brethren of the congregation, as God has prospered you, so offer freely." Persons of distinction would respond first, followed by the elders. One by one the men of the congregation would go forward with their offerings, taking them to where the deacon was seated and depositing them in a box provided for the purpose; or if other chattel was contributed it was placed before the deacons, after which the individual would return to his seat.

III. THE BAPTISTS

Banished from the church at Salem in the Massachusetts Bay Colony, Roger Williams with a few of his followers journeyed southward to Rhode Island. At the site which he named Providence, Williams was baptized by immersion. He then baptized ten others and thus was formed the First Baptist Church in America in the year 1838. Others joined the group at Providence, including a family from the Rev. John Cotton's Congregational church.

As the Baptist work enlarged, the most important center became Philadelphia. There in 1707 the first Baptist association in America was organized consisting of five churches.

The initial attempt of the Philadelphia Association to secure funds from Baptist churches seems to have taken place in 1750. The Association minutes of that year reveal that an effort was made to interest congregations in establishing "a public fund or stock in the bank, well regulated," into which "yearly sums" could be contributed as the Lord had prospered.

This was a rather extraordinary proposal, for the records of the Association mention no special projects needing financial support. At that time, however, the Association was little more than a council or committee expressing fellowship and merely offered advice. This proposal to accumulate a fund for an undefined need produced no results as far as the records show.

In 1755 the Association sent two preachers to visit North Carolina as missionaries. Their appointment carried the stipulation: "The several churches to contribute to bear their expenses." The result was not reported.

In 1790 a pastoral letter was sent out which included reference to the duty of the believers to afford their pastors with a "competent supply of the necessities and conveniences of life," so that their hands would be strengthened for the Lord's work and their minds relieved of perplexity. The letter admonished congregations to "provide houses decent and convenient for the public worship of God." Scriptures were cited to stress the Christian's duty to help the poor in general and "needy brethren and sisters" in particular.

Dr. David Benedict in his volume: *Fifty Years Among The Baptists*, published in 1860, decried the lack of church support of the early Baptist ministers. He alleged that the majority of them had no settled income but were forced to provide for themselves and charged that "the Baptists were more parsimonious in their doings in this line than almost any other party in the country." He further maintained that in cases where moderate sums were pledged, "in too many they were slowly paid, if paid at all."

IV. The Presbyterians

One of the largest nationality groups in the colonies at the opening of the American Revolution was the Scotch-Irish. Their immigration here marks the beginning of Presbyterianism in America.

Concerning the support of Presbyterian ministers, Richard Webster in his volume: *A History of the Presbyterian Church in America,* published 1857, wrote that many of the congregations furnished their ministers with a house and farm, or else promised in the call a sum of money to buy a plantation. The specified salaries, he said, were "mostly paid in kind, wheat, Indian corn, hemp, and linen yarn"—but that "every imaginable article" was also received in payment of stipend.

The general attitude of the early Presbyterians regarding the matter of securing compensation for their ministers appears in a decision of the presbytery of Donegal as found recorded in their minutes of October, 1770. The practice of providing support for Gospel ministers was upheld as "highly rational and warranted by ye Sacred Scriptures." The best method was to be determined by each congregation. It was suggested that in the formative stage of a new church the minister should not expect support.

Before the year 1760 any congregation calling a full time minister was expected to have subscriptions that would assure compensation in the neighborhood of sixty pounds, the equivalent of $300, annually. After 1760 a noticeable increase in the standard of compensation was apparent among Presbyterians until some ministers received as high as a hundred and fifty pounds annually.

Payments were made either in currency or in produce. Renting pews was the most common method of obtaining funds. The most desirable pews, usually those located near the pulpit, brought the largest returns. When subscriptions and pew rents did not bring sufficient revenue, other methods were devised such as lotteries, donations and bequests.

V. The Methodists

The Methodist Episcopal Church in America had its origin in the work of lay ministers supervised by John Wesley from England. In either nation the denomination began as a movement within the Anglican Church. Not until the close of the Revolutionary War was it organized as a denomination.

The first recorded contribution of American Methodists for foreign missions was in 1784 when an amount of $325 was applied to the support of three missionaries outside the United States.

By 1799 there were two hundred and sixty-nine "traveling" preachers in the Methodist ministry, in addition to the eight hundred and fifty "located" preachers. Methodist preachers received an average of $64 per year. Bishop Asbury allegedly favored keeping the wages of his traveling ministers at a minimum for fear that prosperity would encourage them to marry and settle down. In 1839 Nathan Bangs, the Methodist historian, criticized Bishop Asbury's administration. He regarded the defect to be a lack of encouraging the people to make provision for their ministers, especially those with families. The Bishop's fear, according to Bangs, was that if these ministers were "too well off" in material goods they would "lose their zeal and spirituality." As a result adequate compensation was withheld by many congregations and Bishop Asbury was often quoted to justify this failure.

The Bishop had a transcendent view of the ministry and was zealous to prevent "catastrophe" which would come upon the church by the substitution of a "located" for a "traveling" preacher. He, therefore, regarded it essential to keep them aloof from the world by preventing the accumulation of property. The question raised by the above-mentioned historian was whether a minister would not be more induced to locate from fear of poverty than desire for competency. His verdict was that adequate support of itinerant ministers and suitable education for their children would result in a stronger denomination as well as spiritual development and general prosperity.

VI. OTHER DENOMINATIONS

The subject of church support in the early days of the five major denominations, as traced in this chapter, is typical of the various other denominations and thus further interpretation is unnecessary.

CHAPTER II
THE RISE OF MODERN MISSIONS

SPIRITUAL deadness characterized the American churches for a decade and more following the Revolutionary war. One church historian described the period from the close of the Revolution until 1812 as one of "suspended animation." Another, William Warren Sweet, referred to it as "the lowest ebb-tide in the history of American Christianity." It seems that organized Christianity in the United States did little more than maintain itself during this interval between wars. The old adage that the darkest hour just precedes the dawn again proved true. The nineteenth century opened with momentous events for Christianity and of special importance to the stewardship cause.

I. EARLY BEGINNINGS

The modern organized missionary movement was inaugurated in Britain in 1792 when The English Baptist Missionary Society was formed with William Carey being sent to India as the first missionary. Carey regarded all of life as a stewardship and lived for the one purpose of making Christ known to the perishing masses of India.

Three years later the London Missionary Society was launched by the Presbyterians and Congregationalists along with a number of adherents of the Church of England. Similar societies originated in the Netherlands and Scotland.

The spirit of missions soon spread to America. The New York Missionary Society was formed in 1796 composed of representatives from the Presbyterian, Dutch Reformed and Baptist churches with the purpose of carrying the gospel to the southern Indians. In 1798 the Missionary Society of Connecticut was organized by the Congregationalists as a local effort "to Christianize the heathen in North America, and to support and promote Christian knowledge in the new settlements within the United States." At least eight other societies were formed in the New England states with numerous local auxiliaries such as the Massachusetts Missionary Society which was supported by the "Boston Female Society for Promoting the Diffusion of Christian Knowledge;" and "The Cent Institution" supported by Boston women who promised to pay one cent a week for the purchase of Bibles, hymn books, catechisms, and other literature.

19

Organized missionary effort among the American Presbyterians began with the incorporation in 1799 of the General Assembly which received authority to retain property for religious and charitable purposes. Three years later a standing committee on missions was appointed to supervise the work of the missionaries. Previously missions were supported by individual churches, presbyteries, and synods, with the latter sometimes organizing as missionary societies. An example was the synod of Pittsburgh which in 1802 formed the Western Missionary Society "to carry the gospel to the Indians and interim inhabitants." Dutch churches also began to manifest an interest in missions and supported six missionaries in upper Canada.

The Baptists had a missionary purpose even before the formation of formal societies. Missionaries were supported by individual churches and associations as early as 1778, when the Warren Association of the New England Churches commissioned workers. With the dawn of the nineteenth century the Massachusetts Baptist Missionary Society emerged. Being active, it was soon publishing a magazine.

II. The Appeal of the Andover Students

American interest in foreign missions was greatly stimulated by the dramatic appeal of a group of students at Andover Theological Seminary in 1810.

Samuel J. Mills, the leader, developed his interest in foreign missions when Samuel Hopkins, minister of the First Congregational Church of Newport, Rhode Island, endeavored to send two young negroes to Africa as missionaries. Mills came to Williams College having heart aflame with zeal to take the gospel to non-Christian lands. Through his testimony several other students confidently pledged to devote their lives to missionary service. After graduation, most of this dedicated group entered Andover Theological Seminary where three other individuals joined their ranks, namely: Adoniram Judson, Samuel Newell and Samuel Nott, Jr. Their intense desire to engage in missionary work reached its climax in 1810 when they addressed a petition to the General Association of Massachusetts calling for the creation of a foreign mission endeavor and offered themselves as its first missionaries.

The time was providentially ripe for such an appeal, for immediate steps were taken by the Association to carry out this recommendation. The American Board of Commissioners for Foreign Missions was formed June, 1810.

Response from Christians was immediate and liberal. Four wealthy supporters contributed $7,000. Auxiliary societies sent

$4,000 and in 1811 a legacy of $30,000 was received. The blessed result was that in 1812 five young men were ordained in Salem, Massachusetts, and soon set sail for India.

III. THE BAPTISTS ORGANIZE

The emergence of the Baptist foreign missionary organization was remarkable. On the long voyage to India, two of the missionaries sent out by the American Board, Adoniram Judson and Luther Rice, though sailing on different vessels, through study of the Scriptures both changed previous convictions and embraced Baptist principles. After reaching their destination they were baptized by immersion at the Baptist Church of Calcutta. The announcement of their conversion to Baptist views and offer to serve as Baptist missionaries was accepted as providential by Baptist leaders in America. Rice returned to the United States to appeal for Baptist support while Judson went to Burma to establish the first Baptist mission. Rice assumed his new challenge of awakening American Baptists to their missionary responsibility supplemented with appeals for immediate response. As a result of his efforts a committee met in the Second Baptist Church of Boston on May 14, 1814, to inaugurate the foreign missions movement and four days later in Philadelphia the committee completed organization and the General Convention of the Baptist Denomination in the United States for Foreign Missions became a reality. Its constitution declared the objective to be direction of "the energies of the whole denomination in one sacred effort for sending the glad tidings of salvation to the heathen, and to nations destitute of the pure gospel light." Meeting once every three years, the convocation became popularly known as the "Triennial Convention." The formation of this missionary society was notable not only as the first Baptist Foreign Missionary Society but also because of the fact that it was the first general organization of Baptists in the United States. Luther Rice became what today might be entitled as field secretary until the end of his life and he frequently traveled throughout the country promoting missions and education.

At the Triennial Convention meeting in 1817 plans were laid for establishing home missions in the West. John Mason Peck and James E. Welch were sent to the Missouri territory. Although his support was discontinued shortly thereafter, Peck remained in the West to devote the remainder of his life to missions and education. The Massachusetts Baptist Missionary Society supported him after 1820 with a beginning salary of five dollars per week while he worked. In 1832 Peck was instrumental in founding the American Baptist Home Mission Society.

Baptist work among the Indians began when Isaac McCoy was appointed missionary to the Indians of Indiana and Illinois. In 1820 McCoy opened a mission at Fort Wayne where he conducted a school for English and French Indians and Negroes. Two years later he established a mission in southern Michigan named in honor of Carey. There he and his wife labored for four years amidst privation and sickness. The sacrificial effort was crowned with success. From 1820 onward the evangelism of the Indians received great impetus as a result of the Federal government's announced policy of distributing an annual subsidy of several thousand dollars among the established societies engaged in missionary work among the Indians.

IV. OTHER MISSIONARY DEVELOPMENTS

The American Board of Commissioners for Foreign Missions was Congregational in its origin but became interdenominational by the election of Presbyterians to its board in 1812 and four years later Dutch Reformed representatives were added. During the first thirty years of its existence the Board sent out 694 missionaries. One of the most notable of its early achievements was the evangelization of the Hawaiian Islands begun in 1820 which five years later resulted in adoption of the Ten Commandments as the basis of the Islands' laws.

The first home missionary organization on a national scale was the American Home Missionary Society, which like the American Board for Foreign Missions was interdenominational in character. This society became the principal agent in carrying out the Plan of Union of 1801. At first the society was largely Presbyterian in membership but later as numerous local Congregational societies became subsidiaries a large proportion of the missionaries sent to the West were young men from Congregational colleges and seminaries. The society did outstanding work in planting Christian institutions throughout the West and in addition supported struggling churches in nearly every section of the country. Nine years following its formation the society was employing 719 agents and missionaries of which 481 were settled pastors or "stated supplies" with single congregations, while 185 were placed in charge of two or three congregations. The remaining 50 were employed in larger districts.

The Methodist Episcopal Church organized its missionary society in 1819 and The Protestant Episcopal Church in 1828. In both denominations the societies served the dual purpose of home and foreign mission agencies.

The spirit of sacrifice and devotion to the cause of missions is illustrated by the "Illinois Band," a group of eleven Yale

Divinity School students who in 1828 united behind the pledge to seek service in Illinois as teachers and ministers. Only one of the number failed to go to Illinois immediately upon graduation under the auspices of the American Home Missionary Society. A number became ministers and the others established Illinois College.

Interest in missions, both foreign and home, gave rise to many kindred organizations. The increased demand for missionaries led to the establishment of schools where adequate training could be provided. To aid in this important enterprise Education Societies were formed. A national organization known as the American Education Society was organized in 1815 with the stated purpose of helping "all pious young men, of suitable talents, who appear to be called to preach Christ, and who belong to any of the evangelical denominations." In 1818 Protestant Episcopalians established their denominational education society and later Baptists, Methodists and others did likewise.

To this period also belongs the establishment of the first theological seminaries, as well as the first Baptist and Methodist colleges. From 1818 to 1840 the various denominations established at least twenty-five theological seminaries.

The religious destitution of the frontier and the dearth of Bibles and religious literature in the cabins of the early settlers, prompted the establishment of organizations in the East to print and distribute Christian literature. When Samuel J. Mills made his early missionary tours of the United States, covering nearly ten thousand miles between 1812 and 1815, he published a pamphlet reporting the tragic conditions. At Kaskaskia, then the capitol of the Illinois Territory, he found only five Bibles among one hundred families. Even the older settlements of the country suffered sorry shortages of Scriptures. Such urgencies led to the founding of the American Bible Society in 1816 enlarging the type of ministry carried on by the few local Bible distribution organizations which functioned for several years previously. In 1829 and 1830 the Society conducted a systematic program to place the Bible in every home throughout the country with simultaneous efforts being made to supply foreign immigrants with a copy of the Bible at the time of entering the United States ports.

In 1825 a kindred publication organization was formed in New York known as the American Tract Society. The board was composed of ministers representing several orthodox church bodies. Within thirty years there were 659 colporteurs at work under its auspices.

This interdenominational flow of literature was soon supplemented by denominational publication and distribution of literature. The oldest of the church publishing houses was the Methodist Book Concern, established in New York in 1789. Every Methodist circuit rider became an agent for disseminating its publications. In 1824 the Baptist Tract Society was instituted and reorganized in 1840 as the American Baptist Publication Society. Eventually all of the denominations had their individual publication societies and Christian literature was diffused to every corner of the land.

The Methodists seem to have been the first to introduce Sunday Schools into the United States, having done so as early as 1786. The idea spread and in 1824 a movement started which culminated in the creation of the American Sunday School Union. A resolution was adopted by the organization in 1839, with regard to the West, to establish a Sunday School in every neighborhood not having one. Three years later the same objective was set forth for the Southern states. Great effort was expended to carry out the resolutions. Substantial sums were collected and new schools were established. Many agents and missionaries were employed to travel throughout the country for the purpose of visiting the Sunday Schools and setting up still others.

CHAPTER III

CHRISTIANS BEGIN TO THINK
IN TERMS OF STEWARDSHIP

Missions and stewardship are partners. One cannot be mission-ary minded without thinking of life and possessions in terms of stewardship. On the other hand when a person embraces the tenets of stewardship he will likewise develop concern for the needs of a dying world and see the duty of investment to meet that need if at all possible.

In view of the fact that there is such a close relationship be-tween missions and stewardship it is understandable that the rise of the modern missionary movement in America gave im-petus to the stewardship concept.

It is only natural that this should be true. The missionary enterprise challenged Christian leaders with the realization of the great need, financial and spiritual. The effect was a re-examination of the Scriptures with the intention of seeing what was taught regarding the relation of man to his money. The result was Stewardship, the American contribution to theological thinking. It is the purpose of this chapter to trace some of the earliest inquiries into the field of stewardship.

I. MISSIONS CREATE A NEED

The advance of the missionary enterprise increased the need for finances. This will be noted in a probing of the early records of discussions in that period.

The minutes of the Philadelphia (Baptist) Association contain significant remarks of Doctor Furman in connection with the founding of the Baptist denomination's missionary arm, known as the "Triennial Convention." He called for heartfelt consider-ation of the Christian's obligations such as would give an im-pulse to action that with God's grace no difficulties could retard nor any opposition could withstand. Ministers were admonished to offer themselves and the man of wealth "who values the glory of Emmanuel and the salvation of souls more than gold" was invited to give "in proportion as God has bestowed on him." The widow's mite was welcomed if it could be spared.

A circular letter was also sent out by the Philadelphia Associa-tion with detailed analysis of the subject of giving, stressing that the believer is "under solemn obligations to impart a suitable portion" of his material goods for religious and charitable purposes. The letter suggested that the individual should regard giving as "performing an act of worship to God." Note that Christian giving was presented as obligatory, proportionate, and an act of worship.

An editorial in the Baptist Missionary Magazine in 1833 posed the question if it were true that the liberty of the dispensation of grace leaves men free to give what they will, God thereby relying on the generosity of the human heart when previously He required a "fixed amount" of the Jewish people. Proportionate giving was suggested for Christians also when the editorial asked if it were noble to give less than they. The concluding recommendation was that "a definite worthy portion" should be set apart — an apparent reference to the tithe as a minimum standard for Christian giving.

II. SERMONS AND WRITINGS ON STEWARDSHIP

One of the earliest recorded sermons on the subject of stewardship is that of the Rev. Leonard Bacon, pastor of the First Church (Congregational), in New Haven, Connecticut, who in the year 1832 delivered a message entitled: "The Christian Doctrine of Stewardship." Using as his text Acts 9:6, "Lord, what wilt thou have me to do," the preacher asked: "What is the right use of property on Christian principles?" His answer was that the Scriptures obligate every man to regard all of his property and income as belonging to God with himself to hold and manage it "as a sacred trust for which he must give an account to the supreme proprietor." The work of the Lord was to have exclusive priority.

The oldest book on stewardship found by the writer is entitled *The Philosophy of Benevolence* and was published in the year 1836 by the Rev. Pharcellus Church who later distinguished himself as pastor of the First Baptist Church of Rochester, New York. The preface designates the book "for men who desire to subjugate their physical existence to the higher sanctions of reason and divine revelation." The author attempted to condense the true reasons for benevolence and analyze the Scriptural principles involved. The volume was a pioneer in its field. The following selected chapter captions are indicative of its contents: "Vindication of Systematic Benevolence," "Alarming Consequences of Having a Passion for Wealth Predominant," "The Proportion of our Income Which we are Bound to Devote to God," and "Doctrine of Entire Consecration."

Charles G. Finney was at the height of his evangelistic career during the decade following 1825. He was a strong exponent of stewardship. His sermon entitled *Instruction to Young Christians* stressed that converts should be taught that unless they have "renounced the ownership of their possessions, and of themselves . . . they are not Christians." Finney warned against permitting a convert to feel that anything was his own whether time, property, influence, faculties, body, or soul. Conversion meant they had submitted to God and thus made a free surrender of all for God's use and pleasure. "They have no right to spend one hour as if their time was their own. No right to go anywhere, or do anything, for themselves, but should hold all at the disposal of God," said Finney. In his *Lectures to professing Christians,* delivered in New York City, Finney set forth seven accountabilities of men as God's stewards, namely: use of time; talents; the influence exerted on one's contacts; manner of using possessions; one's soul; the souls of others; and the sentiments maintained and propagated.

III. THE SPIRIT OF SACRIFICE ON THE PART OF MISSIONARIES

The spirit of sacrifice on the part of missionaries was a vital factor in promoting the idea of stewardship in the early part of the nineteenth century. Adoniram Judson, the American Baptist missionary pioneer to Burma, serves as an example. Judson held that his life belonged to the missionary cause on the basis that it provided his living. He retained nothing of the considerable funds that came to him from other sources such as money received from the British government for invaluable service rendered as an interpreter and translator. In 1828 he wrote to the Triennial Convention renouncing his possessions and turning them over to the board. He explained in the letter that when he left America he had in his possession a considerable sum of money consisting of personal earnings as well as gifts of relatives and friends. The money accumulated interest for many years and with occasional accessions from other quarters it now amounted to twelve thousand rupees or six thousand dollars. Judson wrote: "I beg now to present it to the board, or rather to Him that loved us and washed us from our sins in His own blood." Four months following this sacrifice of lifetime savings Judson and his colleague, Johnathan Wade, burdened by the pressing needs of the field wrote to the secretary of the American Baptist Board of Foreign Missions offering one-twentieth of their allowance and suggested that a similar proposal be made to the Baptist ministers in the United States. Judson and Wade promised that as soon as one hundred ministers made this pledge to transmit to the treasurer one-twentieth of their regular income they would in turn add a second twentieth, thus giving one-tenth to the cause of Baptist missionary endeavor. Within less than a year Judson proposed to reduce his salary by an additional one-fourth, his "mode of living" enabling him to do so, with the stipulation that the arrangement should not interfere with the previous proposals for devotion. News of this action as well as the consecration of Carey and his associates when published in America gave stimulus to the cause of stewardship.

IV. Laymen Catch the Spirit

A letter from "An Unknown Friend" who sent a contribution for missions appeared in the January, 1830, issue of *The Baptist Magazine*. The content is typical of the spirit of many missionary-minded laymen of that day. The writer mentioned that three years previous he was "impressed with the duty of contributing to missions and other religious purposes" and so designated a certain per cent of his income. The first year he was enabled to give five dollars. God prospered him and the following year he doubled the sum. Finally he doubled the percentage and consequently could give twenty dollars.

In the May issue of this same Baptist periodical was reproduced a letter from "A Georgia Planter." Enclosing ten dollars he referred to it as "a mite" for missions he earned from a cotton field where he had worked hard. "Don't you think that Christians by and by, will act more like stewards with the property God has given them?" asked the planter. "Will not God at a future day require the property he has loaned us?" he added. He complimented Northern Christians for their consciousness of duty and the exertions made to advance the Redeemer's cause. The writer felt great improvement had been made over fifty years previous.

Arthur Tappen, the owner of a large store in New York City is a good example of a layman in the early part of the nineteenth century who had caught the spirit of Christian stewardship. When Finney decided to go to Oberlin, Arthur Tappen gave $10,000 for the erection of a building, and for many years paid Finney's salary of $600 per year. He invested in the cause of Christ almost his entire earnings.

Another layman of that day who possibly did more than anyone else to popularize stewardship among Christian laymen was Nathaniel Ripley Cobb. At the age of sixteen young Cobb went to Boston and secured a position as a clerk. He was converted at twenty and joined a Baptist church. A year later he established his own business and prospered.

Cobb realized his stewardship responsibility. His talent for business was to be used for the glory of his Lord. His duty was to use his talent in earning money for the cause of Christ in the same manner that the minister employs every talent for preaching the Gospel. Accordingly, Cobb drew up a remarkable covenant in which he vowed that his wealth should never exceed fifty thousand dollars. To maintain this standard he pledged to give one fourth of the net proceeds of his business as a start. When his assets reached twenty thousand dollars he would give one half of all net profits. If ever he accumulated the equivalent of thirty thousand dollars he would give three fourths and everything above fifty thousand dollars would be destined for God's purposes.

Cobb was twenty-three when he signed this covenant and although he lived only thirteen additional years he was able to testify on his deathbed that by the grace of God he was enabled under these resolutions to give away more than forty thousand dollars. For this privilege he died with a thankful heart.

The story of Cobb's stewardship was printed in tract form by the American Baptist Publication Society and later by the American Tract Society. Scattered far and wide among people of every denomination, it constituted an appeal for stewardship particularly among businessmen.

CHAPTER IV

THE GREAT STEWARDSHIP AWAKENING

THE PERIOD of the forties and fifties of the last century is usually thought of by the historian in connection with slave agitation. It also deserves to be known as an era of great stewardship awakening.

I. THE PROPHETS OF THE AWAKENING

Horace Bushnell, the popular Congregational preacher and theologian of Hartford, Connecticut, who ministered in the period referred to, uttered a challenge which has gripped the minds of thousands and echoes down to the present day. He asserted that only one more revival is needed, namely of Christian Stewardship or the "consecration of the money power of the church of God." "When that revival comes, the kingdom of God will come in a day," he declared.

Dr. Abel Stevens, a famous Methodist clergyman and editor likewise predicted the indispensable stewardship awakening. "A change amounting to a revolution must come over Christendom" with regard to the "relation of Christian men to property," he said, "before Christianity can fairly accomplish its mission in our world." The solution of that question, according to Doctor Stevens, was the next great duty of the church.

Lyman Abbot, the successor of Henry Ward Beecher in Brooklyn, said that the objective of all business as well as every other activity is the "promotion of the kingdom of God." Abbot was confident that if a man was working with that motive in mind he could be assured of God's help, not merely a financial success but "a means for the service of God and the enrichment of humanity."

The Rev. Josiah Strong, minister of the Central Congregational Church of Cincinnati also expounded stewardship. He made this rather arresting statement: "it is the duty of some men to make a great deal of money." He pointed out that God gave some men money-making talents and to bury that talent is as wrong as to bury a talent for preaching. "Christians have but one business in the world," declared Strong, and that is the expansion of Christ's kingdom. He emphasized that a man in any occupation is "under exactly the same obligation to be wholly consecrated to the work as is the missionary."

II. The Prize Essays and other Literature

Thoughtful ministers and laymen of the eighteen forties and fifties developed strong convictions that the custom of taking "collections" to provide even basic necessities was pitifully inadequate and hopeless for furnishing needed funds for world evangelization. They concluded that people must realize the ethical basis for giving and the underlying Scriptural significance of ownership if their narrow views of benevolence were to develop into the broader aspects of Christian Stewardship.

With this objective in view a unique movement was launched. Several generous laymen enabled tract societies in America and in Great Britain to offer liberal cash prizes for the best brief treatises on the subject of systematic beneficence. The purpose as stated was to stir up the interest of the churches to a more thorough study of the Christian principles of stewardship.

The leading denominations participated in the movement. First prize of $300 was awarded to Dr. Abel Stevens (previously referred to) of the Methodist Episcopal Church for his brilliant essay entitled *The Great Reform*. Second prize of $200 went to Lorenzo White, who contributed a strong Scriptural study entitled *The Great Question*. Third prize of $100 was won by Benjamin James Fry for his incisive essay on *Property Consecrated*. An essay by James Ashworth entitled *Christian Stewardship* received special mention. The winning manuscripts were published by the Methodist Tract Society and widely read.

Meanwhile the Presbyterian, Congregational and Baptist churches of America also felt the influence of this unique stewardship awakening. The American Tract Society which represented a wide constituency among these churches also planned a prize competition, announcing that $250 would be given "for the best approved treatise on the importance of Systematic Beneficence and statedly appropriating portions of income for benevolent objects." The committee of award received and examined 172 manuscripts. Among them were several large treatises. A number were of exceptional value and the committee found it impossible to select one as best. The prize was increased to $400 and four essays were selected as of equal value with the writers each being awarded $100. These essays were published by the American Tract Society and also enjoyed wide distribution, thus making a valuable contribution to the quantity of remarkable literature on Christian Stewardship which was produced between 1850 and 1855 in America.

Private publishers also produced stewardship literature. Books and tracts multiplied. Ministers and laymen in all parts of the country were devoting attention to the broad theme of the stewardship of material possessions, and sermons and discussions on this fruitful topic were the order of the day. A spiritual awakening stirred the churches. Scriptural and ethical standards of stewardship were felt to be the one compelling need of Protestantism.

III. THE GOLD RUSH

In the midst of this experience gold was discovered in California in 1848 and during the next seven years $400,000,000 was taken from the California mines and "poured as a yellow stream into the brimming channels of trade." It appeared that almost everyone was on the verge of becoming wealthy. Newspapers referred to those days as the "golden age." More than ever Christian leaders realized the need of stewardship to protect people from coveteousness.

IV. THE OLDEST STEWARDSHIP STATEMENT

One of the oldest stewardship statements in existence was formulated by the Old School Presbyterians in 1858 during the period of awakening. The General Assembly that year received a report from its special "Systematic Benevolence Committee" concerning the doctrine and duty of Christian Stewardship. "Every man is a steward of God in the use and management of the talents, time, and substance which God has entrusted to him," the statement commenced. The trust must be fulfilled "for God's glory and the good of the world," it continued. Contributions of material wealth for religious purposes with Scriptural motives and manner was set forth as Christian duty and a "part of true piety" as fully as any other spiritual activity. The statement warned that Christians were not at liberty to "neglect or slightly perform at his own pleasure" the ministry of giving. Even more convicting was the committee's judgment that a person could not be a "consistent Christian" and fail to be a "man of beneficence" as well as a man of prayer. Pray and pay go together in the establishment and maintenance of Christ's kingdom. Offering of property to God was summarized as a vital part of early church worship; Christian sacrifice, according to Paul in Hebrews 13:16; a means of grace; a practical phase of our faith to be regularly and systematically practiced; means by which idolatrous coveteousness is counteracted and love of the world crucified. In conclusion the report stated that the "grace of charity" could be strengthened by exercise.

V. THE STEWARDSHIP AWAKENING AND THE REVIVAL OF 1857-1858

At the height of the stewardship awakening the revival of 1857-

1858 swept through the churches. It began at prayer meeting in New York City's North Dutch Church on Fulton Street, called by a lay missionary named Jeremiah Lamphier. Like a match to an "oiled tow" revival fires burst forth. There was no exhortation — no preaching — only prayer. The spiritual impact leaped to Philadelphia, Boston, Washington, Cincinnati, and Chicago and hundreds of other cities and towns throughout the land. Thousands of people gathered in daily meetings with "the voice of prayer as the sound of many waters." The Spirit of God brought poignant conviction to unrighteous men. Professional men and the laboring class alike confessed their sins and entered with joy upon the Christian life. The power of prayer was marvelously illustrated as revival burst forth "wave upon wave over the rejoicing land," using the expression of historian A. L. Vail.

It is significant that this great revival followed on the heels of the stewardship awakening.

CHAPTER V

STEWARDSHIP AND THE PERIOD
OF RECONSTRUCTION

THE YEARS following the Civil War are known as the reconstruction period. In this chapter we trace the varied fortunes of the stewardship movement in such a crucial era.

I. THE DECLINE IN STEWARDSHIP EMPHASIS

The Civil War introduced a new epoch to American life. Steamboats, locomotives, railroads, telegraph and many other inventions revolutionized the manner of living.

Money became more abundant and more dangerous. As H. C. Weber has graphically described it: "Capital shifted from section to section and from hand to hand along the channels of coveteousness, avarice and ruthless selfishness." Men became opportunists in religion as well as statecraft and business.

The four fateful years of war left the nation feverish with ills. The passions of men degraded by the carnel atmosphere of conflict had debased the spiritual standards of an entire generation.

The great stewardship literature produced earlier was permitted to lapse and soon went out of print. *The Great Reform,* another name for the pre-Civil War stewardship awakening, faded into dim memory. Churches resorted to various financial expedients for raising funds. "Money-raising" became a fine art and an essential part of the minister's program. The plan of stated collections with special attractions became the accepted method of inducing churches to give. Thus special days such as "Missionary Day" and "Freedman's Day" multiplied.

The annual budget plan to cover all congregational expenses and benevolences succeeded special collections. In many churches the responsibility for raising "apportionments" became a burden and drudgery. Ministers often found themselves unhappily engaged in a quest for money rather than for the souls of men.

II. THE RISE OF THE STUDENT VOLUNTEER MOVEMENT

The dark post-Civil War setting gives way to a much brighter picture as we trace the events connected with the rise of the Student Volunteer Movement which so greatly aided the stewardship cause.

Leaders of the Young Men's Christian Association movement of the United States and Canada in 1886 approached evangelist Dwight L. Moody who had exerted a profound influence on certain American and British universities and requested him to preside at a special convocation of Christian College undergraduates. He consented. Invitations were sent out for a conference at Mount Hermon, Massachusetts, during July of 1886. Two hundred and fifty-one students from eighty-nine colleges and universities of the United States and Canada responded and remained the full four weeks of the conference. Robert P. Wilder, a young man from Princeton College, along with his sister, Grace, had preceded the event with weeks of fervent prayer. Their burden was that God would call from that assembly of students many to consecrate their lives for foreign mission service. Early in the conference Wilder called for a meeting of all the young men who were thinking seriously of the foreign field. Twenty-one students answered the summons, of which only a few settled the question. This group of consecrated men began to pray that the Spirit of the Lord would turn the conference into a missionary enlistment and separate many young men unto the great task. In a few days their faith was rewarded above their expectations. A special mass meeting was addressed by Dr. Arthur T. Pierson, editor of the *Missionary Review of the World*, at which he supported with convincing arguments the striking proposition that "all should go, and go to all." This keynote provoked thought and prayer.

A week passed and another rally was held, known as the "meeting of the ten nations," which some believe significantly compares in history to the Williams "Haystack Prayer Meeting." The speakers were seven young men of different nationalities — Armenian, Japanese, Siamese, German, Dane, Norwegian and an American Indian — supplemented by messages from sons of missionaries serving in China, India, and Persia. The program was a stirring series of three minute appeals for more workers on the fields followed by a season of prayer. The impassionate pleas came with peculiar force to all. One by one the men, alone before God in the woods or in their rooms with Bibles in hand "fought out the battle with self," and were led by the Spirit to surrender for carrying the Gospel "unto the uttermost part of the earth." The number of volunteers increased from twenty-one to one hundred during the ten days following the "meeting of the ten nations" and the closing session.

On the final day of the conference the volunteers held a special meeting unanimously advocating that the missionary spirit mani-

fested with such power in Mount Hermon should be communi-
cated to the thousands of students throughout North America
who were not privileged to attend. The conviction was generally
held that hundreds of other college young people could be in
fluenced to yield to Christ for missionary service if the challenge
was passed along to them. Four of the group were selected to
visit as many colleges as possible during the year to represent
the Mount Hermon Conference. Of the four chosen, only
Robert P. Wilder, accompanied by John N. Forman, a fellow
Princeton College student, were able to make the tour. An interested layman of Brooklyn, D. W. McWilliams, defrayed the
expenses of the trip. One hundred and sixty-seven institutions,
including many of the leading colleges of the United States and
Canada, were visited and within the year twenty-two hundred
students had signed the missions volunteer affirmation.

During the college year of 1887-1888, in spite of absence of
leadership and oversight for the movement, more than six hundred new volunteers were added to the roster, very largely the
result of personal work on the part of those previously enrolled.

In July, 1888, about fifty volunteers came together at the
Northfield Conference to pray and make plans to permanently
organize the Volunteer Movement. After thorough analysis it
was decided to confine the organization to students and therefore
it was named the Student Volunteer Movement for Foreign
Missions. Robert E. Speer followed Wilder as traveling secretary
and devoted a year to the service, achieving the phenomenal
result of enlisting 1,100 volunteers.

The Student Volunteer Movement had a fivefold purpose,
namely: (1) To lead students to a thorough consideration of
foreign missions as a lifework, (2) To foster this purpose by
guiding volunteers in their study and activity for missions until
they come under the immediate direction of the Mission Boards,
(3) To unite all volunteers in a common, organized, aggressive
movement, (4) To secure a sufficient number of well-qualified
volunteers to meet the demands of the various mission boards,
(5) To create and maintain an intelligent, sympathetic and
active interest in foreign missions on the part of the students
who remain at home in order to secure the strong backing of
the missionary enterprise by their advocacy, gifts and prayer.

The Student Volunteer Movement accomplished a notable
task and from the company of enrolled volunteers over 16,000
went to the mission fields under the auspices of the various
Mission Boards. Scores of thousands of students of North America
were influenced to study Christian Missions. New missionary

libraries and special missionary sections in existing libraries were established in more than 400 colleges and seminaries. The movement possibly did more than any other agency to usher in modern mission study activity. Between sixty and seventy missionary books and brochures were produced under its auspices.

The stewardship emphasis of the Student Volunteer Movement brought about a substantial increase in the amount of investment in missions. Scores of institutions were influenced to individually undertake the support of a missionary.

John R. Mott has stated that the dominant note of the movement was the recognition of the Lordship of Jesus Christ and emphasis on the principle of self denial. This concept, he believed, has done more to give reality and depth to the Christian experience than any idea which has been impressed upon students. "It has thus afforded a challenge to every Christian student for testing his devotion to Christ," observed Mott.

III. Two Significant Stewardship Writings of this Period

Though stewardship literature produced during the period of reconstruction is scarce, two works are worthy of special mention. William Speer, for many years the secretary of the Presbyterian Board of Education, published a book in 1875 entitled *God's Rule for Christian Giving.* It is an exposition of I Corinthians 16:2 which reads: "Upon the first day of the week let everyone lay by him in store as God hath prospered him." He separated the text into four points which define Christian giving as: A weekly religious duty; of universal obligation; by acts of personal consecration and donation; according to some definite end, with the blessing of God, enlarging proportion of the income.

We briefly summarize Speer's convictions concerning the Divine Rule for Christian Giving as enlarged upon in his volume. Its basis is the love of God and complete consecration of everything as an act of worship. Everyone is to serve God in his secular employment, whatever it may be, and gear a portion of the proceeds to the cause of Christ. A certain portion of one's income, not less than one tenth, is voluntarily determined as a minimum standard, with purpose to increase the rate depending on circumstances and as God prospers him. Individuals and families should make their deposits weekly or when the money is received with gifts at suitable opportunities. "Neither the rule as to the rate, nor the collection of the proceeds," warned Speer, "must ever be made compulsory by enactments or processes of Church or of State." A further point of order from Speer was that offerings must not become ostentatious or regarded as meritorious before

God, but reliance must be fully on the "free grace of Christ and his atonement on the cross for salvation and eternal life."

The other work referred to is an address delivered by Rev. Lemuel C. Barnes before the Massachusetts Baptist State Convention which appeared in the November 14, 1889, issue of the *Watchman* and later reprinted in pamphlet form. The message was entitled: *"How to Secure Larger and More General Contributions from Our Churches."* His answer sets forth seven conditions to be fulfilled. The first is that churches require more thorough instruction on the financial phases of religion. It was pointed out that thirteen of Christ's twenty-nine parables have a financial element and often more than a mere illustration. For example, Christ spoke of a "talent" which was a denomination of money as we would say $12,000. The word has been erroneously turned into an abstract noun and then a verbal adjective until the original significance — that a talented man is one who has the power of making money for the Lord — has been forgotten. Secondly, along with deeper Scriptural instruction as to the purpose of money must go a broader understanding of the needs of the world. A third condition is that contributions be made on high principle. Fourthly, offerings should be proportionate. The New Testament terms are clear: "According to that a man hath," and "as he may prosper." The fifth requirement is that the contributions be devotional both in method and motive rather than mendicant or commercial. Christian gifts are acts of worship in their personal origin as well as public manifestation. A sixth vital element is that contributions be sacrificial. The seventh and final condition for more general and generous contributions from the churches, according to Barnes, is that giving be accompanied with gladness and singleness of heart rather than reluctance and duplicity.

CHAPTER VI

THE REDISCOVERY OF THE TITHE

THE PERIOD that marks the close of the nineteenth century and the opening of the twentieth was one which emphasized the tithing phase of stewardship. Previously we find only casual references to the tithe. However, near the close of the nineteenth century, the tithe was unveiled and recognized as a vital means whereby Christians could perform their stewardship. The factors involved in centering new attention on the generally obscure tithing system and its effectiveness constitute the essence of this chapter.

I. THE WORK OF THOMAS KANE

Thomas Kane, a Chicago businessman, was a pioneer among tithers and known to millions through his literature as "Layman." His testimony throws light on the tithing situation in the day in which he lived. He personally did not know another tither until after the year 1876 and of his extensive acquaintance among ministers he could remember none who personally knew a tither.

That year he wrote a small pamphlet on the topic of tithing in which he expressed his personal conviction that God prospers in temporal affairs those who honor Him by dedicating a definite portion of their income to His service. He declared that he had never observed an exception to this rule and requested readers to reply with any information they had on the subject. The pamphlet was sent to approximately three-fourths of our country's evangelical ministers. The replies were gratifying and in 1878 Kane published another pamphlet entitled, *Questions about Christian Giving,* based on the responses received and containing selected testimonies. Sample copies were again sent to three-fourths of the ministers of evangelical denominations with the offer to provide a copy for every family in the numerous congregations. By 1890 Kane had distributed millions of pamphlets on tithing. The mounting cost of printing finally required a small price to cover expenses. The demand prevailed and additional millions of copies were dispersed. No doubt the tract ministry of Thomas Kane was influential in bringing about the rediscovery of the tithe. Before his death a non-profit corporation was formed, named The Layman Company which

41

recently became The Layman Foundation with headquarters in Chicago, and is still carrying on the work of its founder.

II. Tithing in St. Stephen's Protestant Episcopal Church, Manayunk, Philadelphia

One of the earliest cases on record of a church adopting the tithe method for finances is that of St. Stephen's Protestant Episcopal Church in Philadelphia. The parish issued a pamphlet in the year 1877 stating its convictions on the matter of raising money.

"Tithes" constitute the source of revenue of this church, supplemented by the "offerings," said the document, presentation being both a duty and an act of worship. The church wanted to "avoid methods foreign to the Kingdom of God," even if income were curtailed. Members of the clergy were classified as "stewards of God" who "collect for Him, not for themselves" and Scripturally required to live upon what is thus offered to their Lord.

The tithes and offerings were received at St. Stephen's Church "in stationary treasure chests" exclusively and the expenses of the Church carefully estimated from this weekly income with the remainder designed for the rector.

The testimony stated that after more than a year's experience in promoting tithing and "avoiding more popular methods," the church was "thriving and hopeful."

III. Wesley Chapel Inaugurates the Storehouse Tithing Plan

Wesley Chapel of downtown Cincinnati was saved from the fate of closing its doors and instead was transformed into a thriving and expanding church because a number of its members covenanted together to tithe their income. An announcement was placed on the church bulletin board in 1911 or earlier declaring that tithing was the financial plan of Wesley Chapel. "Tithe Covenant Books" were made available at all regular services and adult members were cordially invited to attend the "tithe class" each Lord's Day morning. Attorney Wm. G. Roberts was church treasurer at the time of its financial crisis and suggested the "Storehouse Tithing" plan which the Church adopted. His account of the events is found in James A. Hensey's book entitled *Storehouse Tithing, or Stewardship Up-To-Date*. The substance of the story is that in May, 1895, the Roberts were invited, along with Pastor J. W. Magruder and other officers of the "Wesley Chapel Methodist Episcopal Church" to meet at the home of another of the members for the purpose of considering what could be done to remedy the financial condition of their beloved church home. Wesley Chapel, located downtown, faced grave problems in that its more prosperous members had moved to the suburbs and the surrounding populace consisted primarily of workers and transient tenants whose temporary status interfered with proper instruction in the Word of God. The result was that the once substantial congregation, from both the financial and spiritual standpoint, had been replaced in part by unstable elements.

The Church was fighting a losing battle. Every conceivable method was employed to save the situation, including "suppers, festivals, lectures, stereopticon shows, subscriptions, and the whole round of man-made plans, schemes and devices," with only meager and diminishing returns. The feeling was that if a few more members died or moved away the church property would have to be sold. It was the opinion of those present that every expedient had been exhausted and no better plans could be introduced than those which had already been tried and had failed.

Treasurer Roberts reasoned that God's plan, "Storehouse Tithing," had not yet been tested, in spite of the fact that the eight individuals present professed to be tithers. The point seemed faulty at first but on further examination it was found that "not one had brought all the tithes into the storehouse," but had distributed the tenth widely to the detriment of their church.

Roberts applied the warning in Malachi concerning robbers to themselves, and contended that to remove the curse they must bring all the tithes into the storehouse, which meant their church. He called for decisions from the group and invited them to make a "solemn covenant" with God to practice storehouse tithing henceforth. All responded and Roberts was assigned the task of writing a "tithe covenant" which was later presented to the church and subscribed to individually by the members, following prayer and being convinced that storehouse tithing was Scriptural.

The results of this experiment were discussed in a pamphlet entitled the *Tithe Covenant Plan for Financing the Kingdom of God,* produced by the Rev. E. B. Stewart, a minister of the United Presbyterian Church. He reported that when the plan was adopted in 1895, even though subscribed to by only about one-fifth of the total membership, the Church commenced steadily to increase "numerically, financially, and spiritually." At the close of the year and for the first time in the history of Wesley Chapel every obligation had been promptly settled.

In 1904 the ratio of giving indicated that the tithers gave twenty-four times as much as individuals resorting to other means of contributing. Greater harmony and success was enjoyed than ever before and general benevolences broke all previous records. Subscriptions and extra collections were discontinued. Attorney W. G. Roberts continued to teach a special class on tithing. After nine years of storehouse tithing Roberts informed Stewart that their minister claimed he "never had to devote five minutes of time to the consideration of the finances of the church during the six years of his pastorate." His time could be wholly given to the spiritual work of the church. Prayer and praise replaced merchandise and for the first time in a century of history the Chapel had no destitute or pauper members. This remarkable record was attributed to "the faith of those who kept the covenant" as commanded in Malachi 3:10.

Roberts reported in 1922, after the plan had been in operation at Wesley Chapel for twenty-seven years, that a total of four hundred and thirty-seven indivduals had signed the covenant to date. During those years Wesley Chapel never had a debt and safely endured the financial panics, as well as increasing constantly in numbers, spirituality, and financial ability. "The banner of Jehovah still floats over His little fortress, where His people hold that He is the God of Truth, and never breaks His covenant with those that fully trust Him," concluded Roberts.

IV. OTHER CHURCHES ADOPT THE STOREHOUSE TITHING PLAN

Another pioneer was the Memorial Presbyterian Church of Indianapolis where fifty-five members began tithing in 1898. Pastor F. O. Ballard declared that "the church derived only a small benefit from the practice, because each tither regarding his own pocket as the Lord's treasury disbursed therefrom as seemed good in his own eyes." In July, 1901, seven men began to practice storehouse tithing based on Malachi 3:10, deciding to "enter upon the literal fulfillment of this command and bring the whole tithe into the Church as undoubtedly God's house." They endeavored also to encourage others to do likewise "that God may be honored, and Christ's kingdom may come."

Within the year, there were twenty-seven who anonymously deposited white envelopes bearing the inscription "The Lord's Tenth." The record proved that in six months the white envelopes had brought in nearly as much money as the total amount contributed by the remaining 600 members of the church. Soon there were seventy-five tithers. The result, according to Dr. Ballard, was increased support of enterprises within and outside the denomination as well as generally a balance in the bank. Special appeals, collections and subscriptions disappeared and no auxiliaries engaged in raising money. "It is purely a religious movement based on the Bible and common sense, and is accorded the respect of the community. The spiritualizing effect upon the church is remarked upon," Ballard testified.

Another church to adopt the tithing plan during the same period was the Third United Presbyterian Church, located near the stockyards in Chicago. Pastor E. B. Stewart reported that the forty-six tithers constituted about one-fourth of the membership but contributed approximately three-fourths of the regular offerings and five-sixths of the missionary offerings. The tithe covenant used by the above named church pledged every adherent to compute at the end of each week one-tenth of income from all sources, enclose the money in an envelope not bearing name or amount and place same in the regular offering plate at the Sunday services, or soonest subsequent occasion.

The church was authorized to apportion 72 per cent for current expenses and 22 per cent for the Mission Boards of the denomination to be distributed according to the General Assembly's schedule. The remaining 8 per cent went to various church departments. This covenant relieved the signer from all other subscriptions and pledges. Additional contributions were classified as free-will offerings, thank-offerings, or special gifts with the church treasurer keeping separate account and the member directing the use of the money. Pastor Stewart commented that the eventual goal was distribution of 50 per cent at home and 50 per cent abroad. The covenant was automatically renewed from year to year unless word was received to the contrary. Some individuals chose to make it a perpetual covenant "which is better," concluded Stewart.

V. Societies for Tithers

Near the turn of the century societies for tithers originated. The *Churchman's Tithe Club,* founded in 1896 at Omaha, under the auspices of the Protestant Episcopal Church, was one of the first to be organized. The constitution states that the society exists to emphasize the divine principles laid down in the Holy Scripture with regard to tithing, which they regarded as "binding upon the Christian as well as the Jew" with the promises of temporal blessing likewise applicable. Only that given over and above the tithe was recognized as a freewill offering unto the Lord.

The Society attempted to accomplish its purpose by enlisting as many persons as possible behind the pledge to tithe and promote tithing. In addition it conducted an educational campaign through personal contacts, preaching and printed matter. However, it did not become a large movement.

The signed membership pledge of the Churchman's Tithe Club called for promise to render a strict account to God throughout the year "by giving to the Church and the poor outside my own family, one-tenth of my entire financial income, from whatever source it may be derived."

A tithing society called *The Tenth Legion* was organized in New York City in 1896. It was named after the famous military unit which served Caesar with such unwavering loyalty. The suggestion was that this modern Tenth Legion might fulfill a greater purpose in history than the ancient Roman legion bearing that name and prove infinitely more valuable. Members were to dedicate at least one-tenth of their income to the work of One Who ranks far greater than Caesar.

In April, 1897, the Tenth Legion was taken over by the *United Society of Christian Endeavor* and weekly columns, devoted to the cause, appeared in its publication: *The Christian Endeavor World*. A "certificate of enrollment" was offered upon application to "all Christians that make it a practice, in return for God's goodness to them to give to his work one-tenth of their income." Readers were encouraged to extend the movement among "societies and unions."

By 1902 the Legionaries thus enrolled reportedly numbered 19,490. During this period *The Twentieth Century Tither's Association of America* was organized at a Tithe Conference held in connection with the Winona Lake Bible Conference, August 24, 1904. The chairman of that Tithe Conference, Thomas Kane, appointed the committee of organization consisting of Wm. G. Roberts of Cincinnati, Ohio; Alexander Harbison of Indianapolis, Indiana; and the Rev. W. H. Hubbard of Auburn, New York. An initial membership fee of one dollar and an annual dollar fee was adopted to perpetuate the work of the Association. Every member was entitled to free copies of literature issued or distributed by the organization. Chicago and Winona Lake, Indiana, were chosen as headquarters.

VI. DR. HENRY LANSDELL'S RESEARCH

In the year 1906 Dr. Henry Lansdell issued his monumental work on *The Sacred Tenth,* consisting of two large volumes. The bibliography listed 597 books and pamphlets on stewardship published up to that time, which according to the author was not exhaustive. In 1908 Lansdell published another volume called *The Tithe in Scripture.*

CHAPTER VII

THE LAYMEN'S MISSIONARY MOVEMENT

IN THE early part of the twentieth century another significant movement emerged on the scene which for several years was destined to play an important part in the promotion of the stewardship emphasis.

I. How the Laymen's Missionary Movement Came into Being

In the early part of 1906 the Student Volunteer Movement held its quadrennial convention in Nashville, Tennessee. Nearly 4,000 students and professors from 700 universities, colleges, and seminaries came together for the occasion.

Mission Boards were in financial straits and it appeared that many of the student volunteers would be prevented from going to the foreign fields because of insufficient funds. Thus the officers of the Volunteer Movement invited a number of prominent laymen to attend the convention and to collaborate with the students in the study of the problem.

John B. Sleman of Washington D.C. was one of the men who listened day after day to the powerful appeals voiced from the platform of the convention concerning the challenge of the mission fields. He felt the spirit of the thousands of eager youth who expressed their willingness to go to the mission fields of the world and was profoundly moved. It was then that a strong conviction developed in his mind. He felt that if a program could be designed vividly to portray to laymen of the churches the factors which had influenced the students to dedicate their lives to missionary work, that these laymen would supply the necessary support to send them forth.

During the closing hours of the convention, Sleman discussed the subject with two or three other laymen and in subsequent months, though occupied with business affairs, he continued to present his idea to interested individuals of different denominations. The American Board of Commissioners for Foreign Missions, at Sleman's suggestion, arranged for an interdenominational meeting to be held November 13-14, 1906, in the Fifth Avenue Presbyterian Church of New York City to commemorate the centennial of the famous Williams College Haystack Prayer Meeting, which marked the beginning of the organized foreign mission movement in North America. A group of prominent laymen, influenced largely by Sleman, issued *A Call to Prayer,* an invitation to a select number of laymen of different denominations to come together in the chapel of the same church on the afternoon and evening of the following day.

A severe storm prevented a large gathering. Nevertheless the company numbered seventy-five and was thoroughly representative. J. Campbell White, a United Presbyterian Missionary, who had been brought home to arouse his denomination to its missionary responsibility, was the speaker of the day. He made a deep impression by reciting the remarkable achievements of the laymen, of this, one of the smaller denominations in America at the time. A result of this meeting was adoption of a preamble and resolutions regarding laymen and missions and appointment of a committee.

Open doors to every nation for the Gospel message, highly and efficiently organized missionary boards, and the essentialness of increased participation on the part of Christian business and professional men were stated as basic reasons for resolutions creating a committee of twenty-five or more representative laymen to consult with the secretaries of the missionary boards of all the denominations in the United States and Canada with reference to the following vital propositions: (1) An educational campaign among laymen to be conducted under the direction of the various boards, (2) A comprehensive plan (in conjunction with board secretaries) designed for "the evangelization of the world in this generation," (3) The formation of a "Centennial Commission of Laymen" consisting of at least fifty persons to visit the mission fields and report their findings to the home churches.

In due time a representative committee was appointed which in turn elected the following Executive Committee: Samuel B. Capen (Chairman), Mornay Williams (Vice Chairman), John B. Sleman (Secretary), Eben E. Olcott (Treasurer), William J. Schieffelin, S. W. Woodward, J. Campbell White, Robert E. Speer, and John R. Mott.

II. THE PURPOSES AND LIMITATIONS OF THE LAYMEN'S MISSIONARY MOVEMENT

At the Annual Conference of the Mission Boards of the United States and Canada held in Philadelphia, in January 1907, a report was adopted endorsing the activity and clarifying its purposes and limitations. Recognizing the movement as having been "born of prayer and of the Spirit" the mission leaders accepted it as "another step in advance toward the completion of His great purpose in the redemption of mankind."

The Committee not only saw "evidence of the hand of God" but realized the "imperative necessity" of such endeavor because of "the tremendous demands of a world field, white for the harvest, which requires that the churches of Christendom should lay plans and put forth effort adequate to meet the demand . . . "

The Laymen's Missionary Movement was particularly acceptable to mission officials because of the emphasis that it was *not* a new Missionary Board to collect or administer funds nor to send out missionaries or engage in work outside of regular denominational lines, but rather "a missionary movement of laymen organizing into a promoting agency to facilitate work already under way." It was regarded as a welcome challenge to the existing Boards and Missionary Societies "for larger and higher endeavor," and the pledge of hearty co-operation with the boards rather than contemplation of separate and distinct organizations was definitely appreciated.

The Conference Boards of all denominations thus received the Committee's recommendation of cooperation in securing groups of laymen "to promote campaigns of intelligent, generous interest in Foreign Missions, with special reference to the men of the Church," — the expenses to be carried whenever possible by such groups of men.

The resolution requested the Boards to ascertain from their missions the specific need in men and money "in order to evangelize in this generation the people for whose evangelization they are responsible," and in addition "the provision of the men and the money needed for this purpose," by authorization of the church or churches and the "adoption of such plans as will make possible its accomplishments."

The Committee report was signed by Alexander Sutherland, Walter R. Lambuth, F. P. Haggard, Robert E. Speer, and W. Henry Grant.

III. The Plan of Operation of the Laymen's Movement

The general committee of the Laymen's Missionary Movement consisted of few more than a hundred men who met semiannually. Fifteen men formed the Executive Committee, most of them from New York and vicinity. A monthly meeting in New York City was scheduled.

The Laymen's Movement sought to have organizations in every large center of population with interdenominational co-operating committees to promote an aggressive and adequate missionary policy in all churches of the district.

"Key men" were sought in each local church who would pledge themselves to care for foreign missionary interests, working always with the pastors and church committees.

In parlor and dining room conferences each key man was to endeavor to contact all of the men in his particular local church and to secure as many signatures as possible to the Declaration Card of the Laymen's Missionary Movement, which read as follows: "Believing it to be the duty of the Church of Christ to preach the gospel to every creature, it is my purpose to pray, to give, to study and to work, as God may give me opportunity, that the Church of this generation may obey His command."

The leaders of the movement felt that the time was appropriate for promoting more systematic methods in securing missionary offerings. Men were asked to make definite pledges of money worthy of themselves.

IV. THE GROWTH AND CONTRIBUTIONS OF THE LAYMEN'S MISSIONARY MOVEMENT

The movement spread with great rapidity throughout the United States and Canada. From the beginning it arrested the attention of men on every hand and stirred consciences. Missionary conferences of 3-4 days duration were conducted in seventy-five leading American cities within the year. Largest of halls were filled and pulpits throughout the land were made available. Business and industrial hours were shortened so that more men might attend the sessions. Boards of Trade, Chambers of Commerce and luncheon clubs called special meetings to hear representatives of the movement. Universities, colleges and high schools received speakers. Breakfasts, luncheons and dinners were utilized to reach special groups. The secular press gave considerable space to the campaign. The major conferences held in the larger cities made a profound impression. The Washington conference listed 1,350 delegates; Los Angeles 5,990 and the closing conclave in Chicago over 4,000.

"Every Member Canvass," the use of weekly offering envelopes and careful budgeting of the program of the churches to underwrite their expenses in advance were by-products of the Laymen's Missionary Movement. The canvass had come into restricted use in the nineties but was greatly advanced by the Laymen, who brought it to general notice and acceptance in many churches that previously were unacquainted with the procedure.

The movement greatly enlarged the foreign missionary capacity of many men. It brought them face to face with the Great Commission of Christ. It appealed to the heroic and

the sacrificial. It called to the attention of men their stewardship of the gospel.

The movement discovered, enlisted and trained several hundred new and effective advocates for the cause of foreign missions.
It also developed a remarkable Christian fellowship which
transcended denominational, national and racial lines.

The propaganda of the Laymen's Missionary Movement had
considerable influence on missionary giving. In the three year
period 1905-1907, the Mission Boards of the United States and
Canada received $26,559,806 whereas in the next three years,
1908-1910, they received $33,287,491, increase of $6,727,685.

V. The Laymen's Movement Appoints a Stewardship Commission

In the year 1917, when the World War was in the midnight
of conflict and preceding the launching of the Interchurch World
Movement, the Laymen's Missionary Movement appointed a
Stewardship Commission composed of the following individuals,
many of them leaders in the field of stewardship: Chairman,
George Innes; Secretary, W. E. Doughty; and F. A. Agar, A. E.
Armstrong, W. M. Beachamp, H. R. Calkins, E. L. Carpenter,
F. J. Clark, H. P. Crowell, Ralph S. Cushman, Walter P. Fraser,
Canon S. Gould, Fred P. Haggard, William A. Harbison, J. T.
Henderson, A. A. Hyde, Hugh Kennedy, William E. Lampe,
E. M. McBrier, David McConaughy, William B. Millar, R. W.
Patton, E. M. Poteat, C. A. Rowland, Oliver J. Sands, William
J. Schieffelin, George C. Shane, J. W. Shenstone, Robert E. Spear,
James M. Speers, Joseph M. Steele, John Timothy Stone,
Ambrose Swasey, George C. Thomas, R. L. Walkup, C. E. Welch,
Frederick T. West, J. Campbell White, Bert Wilson and Edward
Woods.

In the February, 1918, report this new Stewardship Commission set forth its Statement of Principles, as follows: (1) God
is the owner of all things. (2) Man is a steward and must give
an account for all that is entrusted to him. (3) God's ownership
and man's stewardship ought to be acknowledged. (4) This
acknowledgement involves the setting apart for the extension
of the Kingdom of Christ, of such a definite portion of income
as is recognized by the individual to be the will of the Divine
Owner.

VI. The New York Office Disbands, but the Chicago Office Broadens the Scope of Its Work

In spite of the success of the Laymen's Missionary Movement,
leaders in international headquarters at New York felt the

mission of the movement had been accomplished, and prayerfully decided to disband its activities — which occurred in 1918.

The Chicago office, however, did not concur with the councils of the New York office and rather than disbanding, widened the scope of its action to influence all the states. The Laymen's Missionary Movement continues its good work out of Chicago to the present. Offices are located in Room 1310, at 19 South LaSalle Street. The movement presently confines its activities to the promotion of *Men and Missions Sunday,* which is observed annually around the 15th of September by over 50 denominations. New workers are being sought and an expanded program planned.

CHAPTER VIII

THE GENEVA CHURCH AND WORLD WAR STEWARDSHIP

DURING the first World War there were significant occurrences in the field of stewardship. Important books were written on the subject during this period. The rescue of the Methodist Episcopal Church of Geneva, New York, from the verge of bankruptcy resulted in the discovery of the outstanding stewardship leader.

I. INTRODUCING THE PASTOR OF THE METHODIST CHURCH OF GENEVA, NEW YORK

One of the men who was destined to play an important part in the field of stewardship was the war-time pastor of the Geneva Methodist Church, Ralph Spaulding Cushman. Born in Vermont in 1879, he received his college training at Wesleyan University and graduated in 1902 with the Ph.B degree. Later, Wesleyan honored him with the D.D. and LL.D. degrees.

Dr. Cushman was ordained in 1902, and served various New England pastorates before becoming pastor of the Methodist Church at Geneva, New York. Following his Geneva experience, Cushman in 1917 became the Secretary of the Department of Stewardship of the Methodist Episcopal Church of America, in 1918 Secretary of the Department of Stewardship in the Inter-Church World Movement and in 1920 first president of The United Stewardship Council of the Churches of Christ in America. Serving as pastor of the Asbury Methodist Church of Rochester, New York from 1920 until 1932, he was then elected bishop of the Denver Area of the Methodist Episcopal Church and in 1939 became bishop of the St. Paul Area of the Methodist Church.

In a message delivered under the auspices of the United Stewardship Council in 1941, Bishop Cushman related the interesting details concerning how he first learned of stewardship in general and tithing in particular.

During his early ministry, a New England businessman who was president of the Massachusetts Sunday School Association interrogated him concerning his preaching and asked him pointedly if he presented Christian stewardship and tithing to his congregation. Cushman confessed ignorance on these subjects, replying that in the little Methodist church in Vermont where he was brought up he had never heard anything about it. The

53

consecrated corporation president asked young Cushman if he believed that his life belonged to God, including his talents, time and money, and that some day he would have to stand before the Living God to account for his stewardship. Cushman replied in the affirmative but with a rather uncertain note and his friend suggested that he put a tenth of his income into the Lord's hands as proof. Cushman rejected the idea at first, feeling that his annual income of $350 was barely enough to support a wife and therefore insufficient for tithing.

He continued pastoring his little church and as he went to the Word of God for subjects he repeatedly found references to money. Finally he determined to face the question. The Bishop refers to it as "one of the greatest hours of my life" when as a young preacher he and his wife got down on their knees and decided by faith to henceforth put aside a tenth of all income for God's kingdom and to acknowledge that everything belonged to God. To this story Bishop Cushman added the testimony: "Now I wouldn't take the habit out of my life for anything you can give me."

II. Cushman's Experience in the Geneva Church

Bishop Cushman authored a dozen books, mostly on stewardship. His last, entitled: *Will a Man Rob God?* appeared in 1942. In it he tells the story of his experience at Geneva.

In the fall of 1915 he arrived at the Geneva, New York, Methodist Church to discover that he had become the pastor of an $82,000 debt. Someone envisioned a new building but did not determine how to pay for these dreams. A large debt, plus considerable deficiency in current expenses from previous years and only a third of the current $12,000 budget in sight after an every-member canvass, with not a single wealthy person in a parish of working men added up to a gloomy situation. Could the new church property be saved? "The answer came from God," related Bishop Cushman, to two men who prayed independently over the situation. The law of the tithe is the test of stewardship. One must take God at His word, bring all the tithes into the storehouse and prove the truth of God's promised blessings. Soon seven caught the vision and consecrated themselves as stewards of God. They upheld their pastor in prayer as on December 12, 1915 he preached on the text: Lev. 27:30 "And all the tithe . . . is the Lord's." Emphasis was placed on the verb.

Pastor Cushman presented tithing as foremost among God's prescribed methods for men to acknowledge Him as Lord of life and possessions and give tangible proof of their sincerity. In their grave crisis God revealed the way to turn defeat into victory.

The tithing plan was presented as "our only hope." Following an earnest appeal for consecration, 125 persons stepped forward, covenanting together with the minister to bring into the Lord's treasury from week to week one tenth of all their income in acknowledgement of their dependence upon God.

On the following night church officials met in conference and adopted a tithing stewardship covenant which was signed by thirty-six of the forty members present. In five weeks 150 people were putting their full tithe into the treasury. Later a second stewardship campaign was conducted and at its close there was a total enrollment of 265. The church was saved!

Within nine months of the fiscal year sufficient money came in to pay all current expenses, missionary apportionments, interest charges, plus a $3,000 payment on the debt. A joyful new spirit possessed the people, which had a widespread influence for good.

The Central New York Conference soon voted to inaugurate a stewardship educational campaign with a goal of "Fifty Thousand Tithing Stewards." A district superintendent was heard to pray, "O God, perhaps we ought to thank thee that the Geneva Church ever was burdened with a great debt, for it was this debt that led the Geneva people to see a great light, and it was this light that led our conference to this great endeavor."

The joyful climax at Geneva came when a group of the church men proposed a "Self-Denial Thank Offering of $15,000" to be subscribed and paid before Christmas, in addition to the tithe. The official board voted for the plan and the congregation subscribed to the amount without hesitation. Before the Christmas of 1917, the entire offering was laid upon the altar of the church.

The writer inquired of Bishop Cushman and was informed that the "Storehouse Tithing Plan" was practiced at the Geneva church.

The Storehouse Covenant, signed by the Geneva tithers, was later reprinted as an official document of the Joint Centenary Commission of the Methodist Episcopal Church and the Methodist Episcopal Church South.

The covenant provided that the full tenth would be brought by the signer into the Storehouse to be cared for by the treasurer of the Storehouse Tither's Association and designated by vote of the association upon recommendation of the Executive Committee. Provision was also made for special direction by the individual "in case of unusual tithe or special divine leading" with such transaction to be kept on the books of the association.

The covenant adherent was free from signing other pledges and all other giving was "free will or thank offerings."

The *Storehouse Tithing Plan* is still in use in many parts of the country. The writer met Rev. Joseph Stumph, pastor of the English Lutheran Church of LaCrosse, Wisconsin, in 1932 and learned that very satisfactory results were experienced there through operation of the same plan. The tithe was deposited in the Sunday offering in a special envelope having Malachi 3:10 printed thereon. Non-tithers used the regular church envelopes. After the service the tithe envelopes were turned over to the Storehouse Treasurer who would record the amounts and distribute the contents to the various treasuries as agreed.

The Storehouse Group in LaCrosse used the same covenant as the Geneva Methodist Church. In addition there was an explanation, which appears in the Appendix for the benefit of readers who may desire to organize a Storehouse Tithing Association.

The largest use of the organized tithing plans probably was in the Wyoming (Philadelphia area) of the Methodist Episcopal Church, resulting from the experience of the church at Geneva. The success of the movement is indicated by the fact that the Wyoming Conference maintained a very high level of giving until the depression.

III. Cushman Becomes President of the Newly Founded
    United Stewardship Council

The story of the organization of the United Stewardship Council of the Churches of Christ, founded shortly after the World War, will be considered at this point because of Ralph S. Cushman's relation to it as the first president.

The impact of the Geneva Church victory carried Cushman to the office of Secretary for the Department of Stewardship during the Centenary Celebrations of the Methodists, and later to the position of Executive Secretary for the Department of Stewardship in the Interchurch World Movement.

In 1919-1920 stewardship representatives of that movement held several meetings and the United Stewardship Council of the Churches of Christ in America emerged from these gatherings. It was formally organized and held its first meeting September 23, 1920. Ralph S. Cushman was elected the first president.

Raising money for missionary purposes was a primary interest but the emphasis soon shifted to teaching the application of the principles and methods of Christian stewardship to life, including the use of money.

The present membership of this Council is composed of men and women from various denominations who have responsibility for the promotion of stewardship in their particular denomination. Other individuals who have unusual interest in stewardship are also elected for a period of three years. The promotion of stewardship in the different denominations follows the methods of operation in conformity with other denominational organization.

Through the years the United Stewardship Council has held some forty stewardship conferences in various parts of the United States involving interdenominational meetings of church officers and local church services and conferences with denominational groups in order that stewardship principles and methods might be promoted in the community.

A set of such principles of stewardship were adopted several years ago and have been circulated by the hundreds of thousands throughout the country. In addition many pamphlets and books have been printed and distributed widely. Numerous study courses have been held in various parts of the country using the books recommended by the Council. A list of approved stewardship books, plays and leaflets is issued annually.

Every year the Council prepares, prints and distributes statistics concerning giving in the various denominations which are universally recognized as an authoritative source of information.

The Education Committee of the Council cooperates with Sunday School publication sources in furnishing materials for the preparation of lessons relating to the subject of stewardship. Special radio broadcasts have also been prepared and carried over nation-wide networks.

The Council has several standing committees, including the Conference Committee, Education Committee, Publication Committee, and the Publicity Committee.

IV. SIGNIFICANT BOOKS ON STEWARDSHIP WRITTEN DURING
    WORLD WAR I

Two outsanding books on stewardship were written during World War I, one by a Methodist and the other by a Presbyterian.

Methodist leader Harvey Reeves Calkins wrote a volume entitled *A Man and His Money*. Bishop Cushman described this 367 page work, which was published by The Methodist Book Concern in 1914, as "one of the best books America has produced" on stewardship. Several editions were issued which did much to influence the thinking of the Christian public toward the idea of stewardship.

Presbyterian leader David McConaughy produced a 187-page volume entitled *Money The Acid Test*. This book was first published in 1918 and soon went into several editions. It is a classic in the field of stewardship and was used as a study book in the New Era Movement of the Presbyterians. This volume also had definite influence on the Christian public and helped make the New Era Movement of the Presbyterians the success that it was.

It was during this period that Bishop Cushman's first book, entitled *Studies in Stewardship,* was published in 1917, and in 1918 he brought out a volume of sermons by representative preachers of the Methodist Church entitled *Stewardship Sermons.*

Chapter IX
THE ERA OF GREAT FINANCIAL CAMPAIGNS

THE PERIOD immediately following World War I was one of un-precedented prosperity in the United States. During the third decade of the twentieth century the wealth of the United States totalled more than the combined wealth of Great Britain, Ireland, France, Germany and the Scandinavian countries. While our country has only 5.3 per cent of the land area of the earth and less than 7 per cent of the population of the world, it had more than one third of the global wealth. The growth of this nation's assets was rapid. In 1850 it stood at 7 billions; in 1870 at 30 billions; in 1890 at 65 billions; in 1910 at 185 billions; and in 1930 at not less than 330 billions.

During this post-war period there was also a great expansion in contributions to Protestant churches and missions. From 1918 to 1927 the foreign mission boards of North America reached peaks in giving never before nor since attained. In the year 1918 the gifts to foreign missions of fifteen leading denominations aggregated $16,482,000, and in the year 1927 they reached $27,179,000. Certain of the leading Protestant denominations conducted great financial campaigns relating to missionary objectives. We shall consider some of these campaigns.

I. THE MEN AND MILLIONS MOVEMENT OF THE DISCIPLES

At their Centennial Convention in 1909 the Disciples of Christ nominated a committee to consider the feasibility of reorganizing the missionary and philanthropic work of the churches. Four years later the first ideal consummated in the "Men and Millions Movement." Activities were carried on during the past World War when $6,300,000 in individual five year pledges was raised over and above regular budgets. This stimulated forward movements in other denominations.

II. THE NEW ERA MOVEMENT OF THE PRESBYTERIANS (NORTH)

A committee was appointed by the General Assembly of the Presbyterian Church in 1918 "to study the presumable effects of the World War on the Churches and to take action to reconstruct the task which had been temporarily inhibited." This committee was known as the New Era Movement Committee. A remarkable financial campaign along with a strong evangelistic, missionary and educational program was inaugurated. The program, begun in the spring of 1919, within the next few years inspired the Presbyterian Church to register unheard of advances in finances and substantial increases in membership.

III. THE NEW WORLD MOVEMENT OF THE NORTHERN BAPTISTS
Following the World War Northern Baptists enlarged their ministry in terms of a five-year New World Movement program. In connection with this activity, the Denver Convention in May 1919 instituted a General Board of Promotion to reconstruct its service agencies. In 1922 Northern Baptists reached the highest per capita giving for total benevolences, namely $7.67 per member.

IV. THE 75 MILLION CAMPAIGN OF THE SOUTHERN BAPTISTS
The *75 Million Campaign* was the greatest financial drive ever put on by Southern Baptists to that date. It was launched in 1919 with the purpose of raising 75 million dollars for the enlargement of the work at home and abroad among Southern Baptists. The money was to be paid in five years. The amount of ninety-two million dollars was subscribed, but due to hard times only fifty-eight million dollars of this amount actually was collected. As a result a debt of approximately six million five hundred thousand dollars was left upon Southwide causes.

V. THE CENTENARY CELEBRATION OF THE METHODISTS
After the World War the Methodists of the North and of the South combined for a Centenary Celebration observing one hundred years of denominational missionary effort. The program was under the direction of The Joint Centenary Commission of the Methodist Episcopal Church and the Methodist Episcopal Church, South. A remarkable response in subscriptions was secured. One hundred five million dollars reportedly was pledged for payment over a five year period.

The Centenary Celebration was launched in 1919 and continued through 1923. Ralph S. Cushman, who was then the secretary of the Joint Centenary Stewardship Department of the Centenary Celebration, announced the objective in the slogan "A Million Tithers in Methodism." In speaking of this aim he explained that the real purpose was "to raise up a million good soldiers enlisted for the Christian conquest of the world."

In a letter to Thomas Kane, otherwise known as Layman, Cushman dealt with the progress of stewardship in the Methodist Church pointing out that a new attitude of enthusiastic support toward tithing stewardship had developed among their previously hostile church editors.

He added that misunderstanding had given place to understanding. Fear of "legalism" gave way to concern about covetousness. Education was suggested to carry Methodists beyond the ABC's of Tithing to the "larger stewardship of all possessions, time and life."

In the letter Cushman reported that about a quarter of a million Methodists had subscribed to a tithing covenant. In addition, he pointed out that thousands of others "increased their giving as an experiment in the matter until such a time as faith dares set apart the tenth." Cushman attributed a multitude of transformed churches and individuals to the effect of the tithing stewardship message. This emphasis he considered "essential to . . . the general reviving of the spiritual life in the churches."

VI. THE NEW WORLD MOVEMENT OF THE UNITED PRESBYTERIAN CHURCH

At the same time that the larger denominatons were conducting extensive campaigns and celebrations, the smaller United Presbyterian Church was promoting the *New World Movement*.

The June 18, 1920, number of *Christian Work,* published in New York City, reported that the United Presbyterians were campaigning for a sum in excess of $16,000,000 as the goal of their New World Movement Fund. Per capita giving was $26.24 the previous year, according to the article. A greater goal than money was to secure 100,000 intercessors, 50,000 family altars, and 50,000 tithers. Church membership then was only 157,135 and 82,000 intercessors were already enrolled. The number of tithers in Young People's Societies had reportedly increased 126 per cent within the year, stated the journal .

Speaking of the tithing emphasis of the New World Movement of the United Presbyterian Church, Dr. J. H. White, then secretary of the Stewardship Department of the United Presbyterian Church, said in a letter to Thomas Kane, that in his opinion "stewardship underlies the success of the whole movement."

CHAPTER X

THE ERA OF CONTROVERSY

THE STEWARDSHIP story in this chapter is not heartening as in some of the other chapters. The period under consideration opened with controversy and closed in a depression. Controversy caused many pastors and laymen to lose confidence in the benevolent enterprises of their denominations. Debts handicapped the spirit of stewardship in many cases. Unified budgets made missionary appeals impersonal. Depression cut the source of income. Thus the entire trend of the period was downward as far as giving to benevolence is concerned.

I. THE INTERCHURCH WORLD MOVEMENT

The Interchurch World Movement had its beginnings in 1919 when many of the Protestant denominations united in an ambitious program contemplating in the course of three years the raising of a billion dollars for home and foreign and other Church Boards. In the year 1920, $336,777,572 was to have been raised, but only $176,000,000 was realized. However, even that was by far the largest amount ever raised interdenominationally in the United States or any other country. Because it fell so far below the established goal, the effort was regarded in general as a failure and even its most ardent supporters recognized it only as a partial success.

The scope of the undertaking of this movement was undoubtedly too vast. Discerning laymen and board executives realized this at the start and urged that the effort, at least during the first year, be limited to the needs of the Foreign Boards. The majority rejected this idea so the new organization went forward with the impossible task of endeavoring to meet not only the immediate needs, but the enormous prospective needs of all the boards.

Inadequate care was taken in the selection of qualified men for mastering the unprecedented and baffling conditions. Leadership was assigned largely to promoter type individuals. Publicity was extreme and often self-laudatory. Official announcements lacked simplicity and clarity. The management earned a reputation for extravagance.

Criticism was also levelled at the scheme of financing the movement prior to the actual campaign. Money was borrowed from banks and certain of the Mission Boards were to underwrite the loan, based on positive assurance of the movement leaders that this part of the fund would be provided by so-called "friendly citizens" rather than the regular church constituencies. Campaign expenses swelled to $8,000,000 and the ambiguous special source yielded less than $3,000,000. The banks came back, of course, upon the Mission Boards, which had to pay the difference. Thus the movement collapsed for lack of adequate finances.

II. The Fundamentalist-Modernist Controversy

A condition characterizing the period following World War I that did much to hinder the cause of stewardship and missions was the fundamentalist-modernist controversy which raged in several of the larger denominations, particularly the Northern and Southern Baptists and Northern Presbyterians.

In the Northern Baptist Convention conclave held in Denver in 1920, a Board of Promotion was appointed which was to coordinate the work of the various societies of the convention and to make one unified budget appeal for the gifts of Northern Baptists. The board was given charge of promotion for the New World Movement. The activities of this Board soon came in for criticism.

When the Indianapolis Convention of Northern Baptists was held in 1922 conservatives began to question the orthodoxy of certain Baptist missionaries reportedly sent to the mission fields. One of the champions of orthodoxy, Dr. J. C. Massee, questioned the Foreign Mission Board concerning its right to send ministers of modernistic training to the field. Dr. O. W. Van Osdel, then pastor of the Wealthy Street Baptist Church of Grand Rapids, called attention of the churches to the fact that only twenty-three cents out of every dollar contributed to the New World Movement was spent for evangelization, while the remainder was used "for civilization, Americanization, and social service." During the 1922 Convention, conservatives tried unsuccessfully to secure adoption of the New Hampshire Confession of Faith by the assembly. A substitute motion, however, was offered in which the New Testament was mentioned as the one sufficient rule for faith and practice.

During those hectic days an editorial appeared in the *Watchman-Examiner* entitled "Our Denominational Situation," which referred to the development of the people along stewardship lines. It described the giving of the churches in general as remarkable and generous for a year of business depression. Missions, education, and philanthropy received $10,000,000, which notable achievement was unfortunately "marred by our heavy debts," said the article.

It is interesting to note that during this period Northern Baptists reached the peak of their giving to benevolences in 1922. From that time on there continued to be a sharp decline until giving to benevolences reached the lowest point in 1936.

In 1925 there was considerable discussion concerning *The Inclusive Policy* of the Northern Baptist Convention. *The Baptist,* which supported the liberal view, sought to instill the churches with confidence in their cause by advocating an inclusive policy on mission fields. It maintained that the Convention did not stand for doctrinal uniformity, but that it laid first emphasis on moral integrity. There should therefore be room for liberal and conservative representatives abroad.

The *Watchman-Examiner* which advocated the conservative view believed that such a confession would "allow some Unitarians, who have an exceptionally high character" but lack biblical beliefs, to work under the banner of Baptists. The *Watchman-Examiner* also pointed out the doctrinal unfitness of some missionaries. The editor felt that sound theology should be one of the prerequisites of a missionary.

In the Southern Baptist Convention during this period controversy centered around the question of evolution. Debts also took the morale out of the stewardship and missionary enterprise. In the *Southern Baptist Handbook* for 1926 Dr. E. P. Alldredge described the mounting indebtedness as an "annoying and destroying factor in the present precarious situation which confronts Southern Baptists." He pointed out that during 1926 alone the total indebtedness on Southern Bapist institutions and agencies jumped from five and one third millions to over six and one half million dollars. Doctor Alldredge revealed that in the South as a whole over 60 per cent of their church members were "almost wholly unawakened, uninformed, and unenlisted" and thousands of leading churches were cutting down the percentages for missions and benevolences of gifts received to twenty-five or even as low as ten cents out of the dollar. The statement concluded with the warning that unless Southern Baptists found a way to "turn back this tide of debt within the next three years, state missions, home missions and foreign missions must largely cease to function."

Southern Baptists reached their peak in giving for benevolences in 1920 during this particular period when they gave an average of $4.39 per member to their various benevolence enterprises. The lowest point in their giving to benevolence was in 1933, when they averaged $.93 per member.

The ship of the Northern Presbyterians was not finding smooth sailing during this period either. Although the New Era Movement produced remarkable results in giving for benevolent enterprises, yet certain phases provided grounds for criticism from the conservative elements. When the New Era Movement came to a close, after its five year duration, the editor of *The Presbyterian* branded the activity as "another of the expensive ephemeral movements which has consumed the Church's time, strength, and money, and revealed their inherent weakness and opposition to sound principles." He referred critically to its passing and the "large legacy of debt" left behind.

III. The Unified Budgets and Their Effects

Unified budgets originated partly because of protests received by the convention concerning the multiplied appeals going to the local churches, and partly because the War brought with it the psychology of big drives. It was still accepted procedure after the War, when nation-wide benevolent movements came into fruition, some of which merged with the Interchurch World Movement. These great denominational and interdenominational enterprises by their very nature spawned unified budgets and plans of promotion. A number of the great boards gave up their personal contacts with constituencies long conserved and cultivated when unification and consolidation of benevolences became the order of the day. It was not only in line with the war and early post-war psychology, but it was related to the developing pastoral uneasiness concerning the multiplicity of appeals referred to previously.

The situation was described by Charles H. Fahs, who in 1929 made a study of Protestant giving for the Foreign Missions Conference of North America under the auspices of the Institute of Social and Religious Research of New York City. Mr. Fahs stated that "specific human needs, the realization of which had been at the roots of benevolent giving through the churches tended to disappear behind the curtain of unified budgets." The tragic result of the shift in responsibility for raising missionary funds from intimate to remote direction was the "insulation" of the missionaries and board officials with relation to church congregations, wrote Fahs. Fewer collections for benevolences and less presentation of the needs to the congregations turned people's eyes toward a *budget* to be raised rather than living realities.

CHAPTER XI

DEPRESSION DEVELOPMENTS

THE ERA of depression may be defined as that period of economic illness which began with the crash of the American stock market in 1929 and continued up to this nation's involvement in World War II hostilities in connection with the bombing of Pearl Harbor, December 7, 1941.

The first part of the depression period was one of great financial adversity. Unemployment figures reached an all time high. The national income declined sharply. Money was scarce. Per capita giving in all denominations suffered a decline.

In spite of those discouraging factors it was an era in which stewardship history was made. Three stewardship plans were inaugurated which will be analyzed in the remainder of this chapter.

I. THE LORD'S ACRE PLAN

One of the significant stewardship developments of our day is entitled *The Lord's Acre Plan* which grew from one successful experiment into an immeasurable movement. The simplicity and adaptability of this plan has resulted in its wide use in rural areas.

A. *The History of the Plan*

The Lord's Acre Plan as an organized movement began with James G. K. McClure, a Presbyterian minister, who went to the North Carolina mountains to regain his health. He became distressed over the plight of farmers around Asheville, whose cash income averaged only eighty-six dollars per year. In 1920 McClure organized a co-operative to help his neighbors raise better crops and tap new markets. He secured aid from wealthy people to finance a broad farm-improvement and educational program.

Later he heard of a church in South Carolina that paid for a new building by having each of their members pledge a few rows of cotton, based on what each person could afford. These parcels of land were called God's Acres.

McClure began thinking that possibly his farmers could *grow* extra income for their churches. Many of the rural congregations were destitute and a little extra income would assist them to carry on. McClure arranged for his co-operative to market produce raised by the churches. He established the only religious department of any co-operative in America and in 1930 persuaded his brother-in-law, the Rev. Dumont Clarke, to leave his Vermont charge to direct it.

That year six churches in western North Carolina adopted the *Lord's Acre Plan,* at least four of which are still using it successfully today. Fifty more rural churches followed suit the second year, of which thirty-nine continue to operate the plan. In 1935 two hundred churches were participating, which number increased to one thousand by 1940. In mid 1943, the Rev. Dumont Clarke informed the writer that there were then between three and four thousand churches using the plan. He explained that since the plan is so simple, churches started it and often made no report to their denomination of their use of the plan. Hence exact figures were not available.

The Lord's Acre Plan has received national attention, being publicized in many magazines both religious and secular, and even via a major radio network.

Many missionaries have examined the plan and returned to apply it in fields such as China, Africa, India, and Korea.

An example indicating how the Lord's Acre Plan has been adapted to the mission field is found in the provisions of a pledge promoted by the *Systematic Giving Board* in Korea for the use of Korean Christians.

Acknowledgment of God's gifts to the individual and God's claim upon his life and time forms the basis of the pledge to his church which is divided into the following categories: *Weekly Cash Gifts,* to be paid if possible at the time of the regular church service; *Harvest Gifts,* to be paid in cash or produce at harvest time; *Labor Gifts,* consisting of days of labor on his own or the church farm, or in some village craft with the income going to the church; *Crops,* on his farm or on that of the church to be tended faithfully and the proceeds given to his church; *Animals,* belonging to the individual or to the church to be fed and cared for and the proceeds given to the church; *Home-Crafts* to be made and the proceeds given to the church. The member was to fill in figures indicating amounts or numbers pledged and affix his signature.

B. Illustrations of Lord's Acre Projects

How to hold the interest of children is one of the church's greatest problems. *The Lord's Acre* helps solve it. For example, the Mills River Presbyterian Church near Horse Shoe, North Carolina, paid off its debt by *Lord's Acre Projects* involving the youngsters as well as the grownups. Francis Burgin, a child of sixteen was fattening a calf as her personal *Lord's Acre* project. Jimmy and Mildred Gilreath, twelve and fourteen, were raising a pig. Jimmy Brown gave one-tenth of his carefully tended 4-H produce. Alice Paterson, six, had various *Lord's Acre* projects since she was two. The first year she earned one dollar with chicks. Another year she raised ducks which sold for eight dollars, and last year she fattened a pig named "Whitey," which brought eighteen dollars at the market. "It was a big *Lord's Acre* Year for Alice."

The Dana Baptist Church near Henderson, North Carolina, in a single year obtained $2,352 through *Lord's Acre* Projects. In February the Dana folk, young and old, selected their *Lord's Acre* projects — decided what they would grow. Some were individual projects and others were carried out by groups; either families or Sunday School classes. Profit possibilities were calculated in advance. A systematic plan was mapped out in the spring and carried through until harvest.

Some men dedicated patches of land to the Lord, planted corn, beans, or sweet potatoes, and turned over the money received in the autumn. Other men fattened pigs for market. Church women contributed their "Sunday eggs" or grew flowers to sell. Little children fed chicks until they were fryers and could be sold.

As a group project the Men's Bible Class raised potatoes, and one man contributed storage space in his barn until a higher price was obtained. A lad picked berries as his project and sold them at the market during the hot summer months to earn twenty-two dollars for the cause.

Joe Chamberlin, writing in the *Christian Herald,* related that when he visited the Dana Church and talked with the people he could "not only see but feel its spirit of accomplishment." The common situation in churches where a few people carry the financial load and perform the duties was not true there for each was doing his share. Dana had a new brick church paid for and completely equipped and a parsonage under construction, with the men contributing the labor.

The *Lord's Acre Plan* enabled the Dana people to march forward where before they stumbled, said one member.

C. How the Lord's Acre Plan Operates

Readers who are interested in learning more about the *Lord's Acre* are advised to write to the Religious Department of the Farmer's Federation located in Asheville, North Carolina, of which Rev. Dumont Clark is director.

The first problem in connection with instituting the *Lord's Acre Plan* is to get it started. Because of its Biblical sanctions

and practical nature it readily commends itself to the people of
the country churches. Good management is needed to insure
success. It must be carried out systematically under the guidance
of the pastor and with "the enthusiastic, intelligent, sustained
oversight of a special committee of the church" as one writer
stated.

The plan should be thoroughly presented at a church service,
at which time there should be appointed the *Lord's Acre Committee,* consisting not only of men but women and a leader of the
young people. The committee should begin active work in
December or earlier to determine the best way to work out this
flexible plan in their particular local church since conditions
vary. A determined sum and a definite object for the proceeds
from the projects, especially one that appeals to the young people
and children, is vital.

A marketable commodity must be selected and when the task
is initiated it should be prayerfully maintained and not abandoned until completed.

Further information on the operation of the *Lord's Acre Plan*
is found in Dumont Clark's pamphlet, *The Lord's Acre Plan at
Work in the Country Church.* He advocates that Sunday School
teachers take advantage of their great opportunity, week by
week, to interest the members of their classes in worthy *Lord's
Acre* projects. A goal, he suggests, may profitably be adopted by
each member of a class and by each class in general. A committee
should seek to enlist all others outside the Sunday School to whom
the church ministers, says Clark.

"The projects should be worthy in size, with the tithe as a
standard," writes the author. He points out that other groups
such as future farmers, 4-H Clubs, industrial workers, and sewing
circles can effectively apply the *Lord's Acre Plan.* Individual
projects are strongly recommended as "daily reminders of God
in the home and on the farm" and a stimulant for individual
responsibility. Family projects are listed as next in order of
desirability with group or class projects also encouraged where
there is good leadership and a spirit of cooperation.

Clarke recommends inspection of the projects by pastors,
teachers and committee to provide encouragement and advice.

Marketing the products demands enterprise since each worker
is expected to sell his own crop for the highest offer.

Finally, says Dumont Clarke, the treasurer should keep a careful record of each project.

D. Spiritual and Material Values of the Lord's Acre Plan

The *Lord's Acre Plan* has wonderful spiritual and material

possibilities. A dedication service is usually held in the early spring, and a harvest or thanksgiving service in the fall. If the programs for these occasions are carefully prepared great inspiration comes to the people. Sometimes an out-of-doors service on Rural Life Sunday is held.

Brief services actually held on "the Acre" and conducted by the pastor or Sunday School teacher, with the recitation of memorized Scripture passages and prayer by the workers holds many blessings. Recognition of the workers as they make their offering of the Lord's Acre proceeds has proven helpful. A *Lord's Acre Hymn,* written by Rev. Dumont Clarke, adds further spiritual impact in those special programs.

The Lord's Acre Plan provides a wonderful means of teaching stewardship to young people. Thousands of 4-H club workers and future farmers through it are learning to set aside a portion of their increase for the Lord's work.

The spiritual and material values of the Lord's Acre Plan were well summed up by Rev. Dumont Clarke on a network radio broadcast in November, 1939.

Everyone in the church and Sunday School has the opportunity to take a daily part and the Lord's portion is set aside from the beginning and not made to depend on indefinite profits. Christian character grows with this daily work for the Lord, evangelism is aided and discipleship is more clearly understood. Total contributions of the church are definitely increased thereby with training in tithing. Farm children are provided the only practical method of stewardship training. The secular and the sacred are brought together on the practical plane. Even the standard of farming is raised, thus benefitting the farmer and his church. Bible teachings concerning service become more vital and closer bonds between pastor and people are established. Interest grows and leaders develop. Church activity is united, fellowship enlarged and the entire ministry of the church is thereby strengthened. Daily work on the farm is brought into closer harmony with Christian doctrines and the rural church bears the fruits thereof.

II. THE BELMONT PLAN

The Belmont Plan, also known as the *Belmont Covenant Plan,* is actually not so much a *plan* as it is an *experience* which was enjoyed by the pastor and people of the Belmont Presbyterian Church of Roanoke, Virginia.

A. The Story of the Belmont Plan

The Rev. G. L. Whiteley was pastor of the church referred to above during the depression and experienced the common problem of many a minister at the time. Hard times took its toll and the church seemed doomed to gradual extinction due to financial difficulties. He was convinced that merely resigning his pastorate would not solve the problems of the Belmont Church. Something more than simply reducing expenses had to be done in order to guarantee the church's continued existence. Pastor Whiteley set out to challenge his officers and people to experiment with the original basis of church support, namely, tithing. To this end he thoughtfully studied his problem, and then went to work.

The pastor told the remarkable experience which followed to the General Assembly of the Southern Presbyterian Church in 1934, of which his church is an affiliate. He pointed out that Belmont had an active membership of 352 and total membership of approximately 425, composed largely of middle class men and women who form the backbone of our nation and know neither demoralizing poverty nor delusive wealth.

Because of unemployment in 1932 and 1933, the church suffered a serious financial condition. A new church built in 1929 at the cost of $30,000 was weighed down with a debt of $15,000 and in 1933 a spirit of defeat crept into the congregation which the pastor referred to from the pulpit as "destructive pessimism." The pastor found that there were at least 120 "dependable" persons out of a total of 137 members having employment and the average weekly income was $18. Thus a total weekly income of $2,160 would produce a tithe of $216 whereas the church had been receiving an average of only $50 a week. Bills amounting to $2,600 were accumulated plus a spirit of defeat. Based on facts and figures, the pastor concluded that if his 120 dependables would tithe for the last quarter of 1933 all deficits could be wiped out and the regular budget maintained.

He called the twenty-seven church officers together to present the tithing plan for their consideration. A heated debate reportedly followed but all except two of the officers signed a pledge to tithe for fifteen weeks. Based on their support, the pastor decided to personally call on 120 members and present the plan. The result was that 118 of the wage-earners signed a pledge to bring their tithe into the church. The period decided on was September 17 to December 24, 1933. When the new plan started the offering jumped to $173 the first Sunday and experienced the largest offering of $450 compared to the previous $50 average. The financial goal was reached within the prescribed period and Malachi 3:10 again proved true with resultant blessings. Some members secured better jobs, reported the pastor. Wages increased in other cases and everyone received spiritual blessings. The congregation was transformed in interest, enthusiasm, devotion and joy. People who previously did "not believe in tithing and could not afford to do it," testified that it was a wonderful experience and that they desired to continue giving the tenth of their income. As a result, reported Pastor Whiteley, when Belmont made its Every Member Canvass for 1934, the budget was over-susbscribed by $2,000 and weekly offerings of the congregation were multiplied by two or three.

B. *The Growth of the Belmont Plan Movement*

The movement inaugurated by the Belmont Plan grew rapidly, having been widely spread via the stewardship literature of several denominations. Statistics, however, are hard to obtain since many churches use this plan or a similar one but fail to make the fact known. Many Presbyterian, Brethren, Methodist, Baptist and Christian churches have used it with marvelous results.

Twelve churches in and around Roanoke followed the example of the Belmont Church, resulting in an increase of $17,000 over and above their usual offerings during the thirteen weeks period.

At the request of the 1934 Southern Presbyterian Assembly, Pastor Whiteley's congregation granted him a leave of absence to relate to other churches in the Southern Assembly the story of their experience. Other pastors who had tried the plan also visited among the churches with accounts of success. Enthusiasm spread widely, so that when the 1935 Assembly met, 686 churches reportedly had tried the plan. A deepening of spiritual life as well as increased offerings were the attested results. The plan was again heartily endorsed by the 1935 Assembly and the churches which had not tried it were urged to do so.

C. *Experiences of other Churches with the Belmont Plan*

Baptist Churches which made tests of this tithing plan have had similar experiences to that of the Belmont Presbyterian Church. The church at Batavia, Illinois, for example, for four months previous to entering upon its tithing experiment had an average weekly offering of $33.20. On the first Sunday after the plan was inaugurated the offering enlarged to $70.05. There were significant increases in the regular gifts of individuals.

The first ten weeks' experience with the plan at the Arlington Street Baptist Church at Akron, Ohio, in spite of handicaps arising from the serious illness of the pastor at the time of introduction, produced increases in giving up to 50 per cent over the offerings of the same dates a year previous. Contrast $311.14 with $212.41, or $393.95 with $187.60.

The First Presbyterian Church of Welch, Virginia, had a membership of 288 in 1934. On July 14 of that same year, Pastor Smiley Williams sent to his stewardship secretary a report concerning the operation of the Belmont Plan in his church, showing that the total receipts in 1933 were $1,554.87 whereas in 1934 the figure grew to $3,666.64.

The Presbyterian Church at McAllen, Texas, had a remarkable experience with the Belmont Plan. They adopted it for fifteen weeks. Offerings had averaged $62.00. The first Sunday under the Belmont Covenant plan brought in $155.21. Only twice during the fifteen weeks did the offering go below $100.00 and one Sunday reached $607.27. The congregation unanimously decided to continue it for an entire year.

The Covenant usually used by Southern Presbyterian Churches in connection with the Belmont Plan first of all recognizes the fact that God is Sovereign Owner of all things and that man is a steward who must give account of all entrusted to him. These truths must be acknowledged in man's life in a material way; namely by setting apart a definite portion, specifically a tenth, of his income as an act of worship and dedicate it to the work of the Kingdom of Jesus Christ. Following this summary of stewardship principles were spaces for signature, address and date.

III. THE LORD'S HOUR PLAN

Closely associated with *The Lord's Acre Plan* for farmers is *The Lord's Hour Plan* for city dwellers who work by the hour. Though actually developed after the outbreak of World War II hostilities, it seems best to relate the matter at this point.

The originator of *The Lord's Hour Plan* is Dr. Ralph H. Jennings, who then was pastor of the Van Brunt Presbyterian Church of Kansas City, Missouri, and later became the pastor of The First Presbyterian Church of Kansas City, Kansas, followed by the position of Executive of the Synod of Missouri with headquarters in Jefferson City.

Dr. Jennings testifies that the plan was "born in prayer and as a result of a great need" in the church of which he was pastor at that time. Early in the fall of 1941 Jennings asked the circles of the women's organization to give a report on the *Lord's Acre Plan,* with the suggestion that if farmers could accomplish so much, why could not city church members do something comparable.

The *Lord's Acre Plan* was also discussed in the Session meeting in December. The sixteen officers present voted to set aside

what they earned the first hour of Monday morning as a special
gift to be presented to the church and designated as the *Lord's
Hour* gift, for the purpose of conducting a church advancement
program. The matter was to be kept a secret of the sixteen
officers for a month. They agreed to remember one another in
prayer on those Monday mornings and at the next meeting
would share their experiences. It proved to be such a blessing
that the session voted unanimously to recommend the idea to
the entire congregation.

Accordingly the bulletin of the Van Brunt Presbyterian Church
for December 26, 1941, carried a front page article concerning
a proposed Lord's Hour Enrollment Sunday the following week.
Communion Sunday was considered an appropriate time "for
the Lord's Supper is a time of commitment and consecration,"
said the announcement. "It can have tremendous spiritual
possibilities for each person participating . . . ," said the
article. The idea again was to covenant with the Lord to contribute the earnings of Monday morning's first hour to the church
and was not to take the place of regular weekly pledges or
offerings.

Suggestions for use of the money were to pay off the $1,500
indebtedness on the church building and purchase new hymn
books. However, a vote would be taken each month by the
session to determine immediate disbursement. When the next
Sunday, January 2, 1942, arrived, selected members of the session,
who with the pastor had already participated in the Lord's Hour
Plan for one month, testified of their experiences with the result
that the proposal was inaugurated by the entire church with over
sixty people immediately enrolling and others indicating a
desire to participate.

Participating in the Lord's Hour Plan proved to be a growing
experience for those who shared it. By the end of the year $2,500
came into the Lord's Hour Fund. However, the pastor asserts
that the dollars and cents received were not the main blessing
in connection with the plan, rather " . . . the fact that practicing the presence of God on the first hour of the week proved to
be a spiritual experience for many of the participants . . . "
and the emphasis was "entirely on the spiritual."

Chapter XII

WORLD WAR II AND THE IMMEDIATE
POST-WAR PERIOD

The two-fold period to be studied in connection with the stewardship emphasis in this chapter is the era of World War II and the years immediately following. During the first half of this period the energies of the nation were consumed in the gigantic task of winning the war. The last half of the period was marked by great stewardship campaigns in several of the larger denominations.

I. The Period of World War II

Even before our official entrance into the second world war, defense production had stimulated our economy until unemployment was virtually eliminated. Along with increased employment and production came corresponding rises in wages and the cost of living. Contributions for church purposes, however, did not keep pace with the increased national income. In fact, the period of World War II proved to be an era of decline in stewardship emphasis. Several factors combined to bring about this condition.

(1) As already mentioned, the energies of the leadership of the nation were for the most part consumed in the tremendous problems connected with winning the bloodiest and most destructive of all wars.

(2) The war brought disruption to family, social and church life. Millions were drafted into the military service of our country. Other millions were uprooted from their established homes to be transplanted in distant places to work in war plants in one of the greatest population shifts in our country's history.

(3) Many ministers were removed from their congregations when they volunteered to serve as chaplains in the armed forces.

(4) The stewardship literature of the previous period had largely lapsed. In addition, few men had the leisure required for the preparation of new literature. Paper rationing and shortages made it practically impossible to publish new literature, especially full length books.

II. The Immediate Post-War Period

The victorious conclusion of the war brought many changes.

The boys came home. Millions of new homes were established. Thousands of new churches were planned and built. The leaders of the various denominations began to realize the importance of gathering larger sums of money for the extension of home missions and for the rehabilitation of the war torn mission enterprises around the world.

To this end extensive stewardship campaigns were launched by the various denominations, in connection with which a great deal of promotional literature was produced to educate the Christian public regarding stewardship responsibilities. Profiting from the experiences of campaign programs at the close of World War I, the present leaders used mostly pledges drawn up on a short time basis, to be paid within two or three years.

Though the main story of what the various denominations are doing in the way of stewardship emphasis is told in Part Two of this volume, the remainder of this chapter outlines briefly the great campaigns launched by some of the major denominations.

A. *The World Mission Crusade of the American Baptist Convention*

In the months immediately following the war, American Baptist Convention sponsored the great World Mission Crusade. In this effort over $16,000,000 was raised for the reconstruction and rehabilitation of war torn American Baptist mission stations around the world.

B. *The Centennial Crusade of the Southern Baptists*

The 1946 Annual of the Southern Baptist Convention contains the story of the launching of this movement. It reports that in 1945, the Centennial year of the Convention, "a special effort was made to worthily complete, celebrate, climax, and crown the century for Christ," entitled the "Centennial Crusade." Six great objectives were listed, namely: "winning a million more souls to Christ; enlisting a million more souls for Christ; teaching a million more souls the Word and will of Christ; rebuilding war's wreckage; reviving scriptural giving; and relieving humanity's needs." The hope was expressed that Southern Baptists would contribute at least $20,000,000 for the support of the denominational program throughout the South.

The report states that all objectives were not realized but that the Centennial year was the greatest recent year in Convention history. Total church contributions for 1945 were nearly 98½ million dollars, or an increase of almost 22 million dollars over 1944. Gifts to missionary causes were approximately 22½ million dollars which was an increase of over 5 million dollars over the previous year.

Although gifts for church support and denominational work were reportedly the largest in their history, still the returns were insufficient to satisfy denominational needs and the program for world evangelism.

The Centennial Crusade was followed with *The Enlarged Co-operative Program* the next year. The Convention Executive Committee in giving authorization for this program stressed six points: (1) "Indoctrination" for the purpose of informing the people on the doctrines, program, and work of the Southern Baptists. (2) "Conservation" to retain past victories. (3) "Continuation" referring to the extension of the Centennial Crusade objectives. (4) "Augmentation" regarding increased support of Southern Baptist boards and institutions. (5) "Cooperation" enlargement of the co-operative program receipts to help provide needed funds. (6) "Debt Freedom," the principle of rebuilding and enlarging only when funds are available. (7) "Stewardship," the objective of enlisting one million Southern Baptist "tithers for Christ."

The *Southern Baptist Convention Annual of 1947* revealed that the results of this *Enlarged Co-operative Program* were very encouraging. A "good beginning" was reported in the tithing campaign in that the various states adopted tithing goals totaling more than one million. Pastors and churches increased their stress on Christian stewardship with the "tithe as the minimum basis of Christian giving" and response was summed up as "very gratifying".

Simultaneous with the effort to secure a million Southern Baptist tithers in 1946 there was authorized *A Special Campaign for Post-War Relief and Rehabilitation* with a special goal of raising three and one-half million dollars during the year. The stated purpose was for Southern Baptists "to share of our abundance with the victims of war," with the relief administered by the Foreign Mission Board.

In the *Annual of the Southern Baptist Convention* for 1947, there appears a report of the victorious results of this campaign for the previous year. A total of $3,743,300.73 was received through the Executive Committee and some additional funds were sent directly to the Foreign Mission Board. The hearty cooperation of all Southern Baptist agencies and goals adopted by every state brought in the nearly quarter million extra dollars.

Within the Southern Baptist Convention of 1947 a crusade for *A Million Southern Baptist Tithers for Christ* was launched for the last quarter of the year. The Executive Committee urged that the program for achieving ten million dollars and one million tithers be stimulated by a special "Tithers Enlistment Campaign" to be the "most intensive and thorough of any that Southern Baptists have ever undertaken."

September was set aside for preparation and October 5 designated as "Tither's Enlistment Day." All churches were asked to endeavor to secure tithers for the ninety-day period remaining in the year.

A special "tither's card" was recommended for use by the people in making their commitments to tithe.

Dr. Merrill D. Moore, the Director of Promotion and Associate Secretary of the Executive Committee of the Southern Baptist Convention, commented enthusiastically on the success of this campaign. He stated that in his judgment "the crusade for *A Million Southern Baptist Tithers for Christ in 1947, was one of the most significant single steps Southern Baptists have ever taken in the direction of stewardship advance." Previously stewardship and tithing were merely preached, he said, but here was the first Convention-wide concerted effort to enlist tithers on a significant scale. He referred to it as the "cornerstone of our programs and missionary advance" and the foundation for the movement entitled Every Baptist A Tither, which was inaugurated in 1948 and made further progress in enlisting Southern Baptists.

A streamer imprinted with the slogan *Every Baptist A Tither,* in the handwriting of its originator, Dr. Louie D. Newton, was distributed to every pastor in the Southern Baptist Convention, and was displayed in almost every church. The slogan and movement "caught fire" and is regarded by Dr. Moore to have been one of the most significant factors in improving the stewardship record of Southern Baptists.

C. The Crusade for a Christian World

The Disciples of Christ during this same period launched *The Crusade for a Christian World.* In this crusade the leaders of this denomination challenged membership to respond to a goal of 500,000 tithers and proportionate givers to be enlisted by June 30, 1950. The program emphasized the local church under three headings — evangelism, education, and stewardship.

The committee reporting on the objectives of the crusade recognized the fact that "the Disciples of Christ cannot assume their rightful place of leadership in America with their present standards of stewardship practice." To meet the "challenge of materialism" requires more than "half hearted programs of stewardship which too often becomes only money raising effects," stated the committee.

The urgency of the world's needs was also set forth as a demand for more adequate expression of stewardship on the part of the people in line with the material resources entrusted by God. A program of "stewardship education and enlistment that will reach every church in the brotherhood," was inaugurated by the leaders.

The goals of the crusade were explained as having two equal divisions — 250,000 tithers and 250,000 proportionate givers. Each state or area was suggested a goal based on the minimum percentages required to reach the national goal; which amounted to 18% of the resident membership to be enlisted as tithers and an identical percentage to be enlisted as proportionate givers.

Easter to Pentecost was allotted in the calendar for the program of activities of the Crusade, and therefore became a period of enlistment.

D. *The Crusade for Christ of the Methodists*

In the Methodist Church The General Board of Lay Activities has since 1940 had for its primary task the promotion of Christian Stewardship. Success had previously attended its efforts but the board felt that much more could be done during the Quadrennium 1944-1948. Consequently, following a series of stewardship study and planning conferences, it presented a memorial to the General Conference of 1944 which called for "a consistent, continuous and unified program of cultivation in Christian Stewardship throughout the denomination with cooperation of all agencies and leaders.

The year 1947 was designated as Stewardship Year for the purpose of conducting an intensive program to culminate in total enlistment of church members for a more complete dedication of their lives and possessions to the principles and practice of Christian Stewardship."

The Over-All Stewardship Objectives for this Crusade were stated as a 50 per cent increase in regular attendance at worship service, a half-million growth of active workers in the church to commit themselves to "some form of training for their tasks; the doubling of regular contributors; enlistment of one-million proportionate givers with at least half of them being tithers; an overall increase of 25 per cent in contributions to all causes of the church or approximately thirty million dollars each year; five thousand for the ministry requirements of the Methodist denomination and an additional five thousand recruits for service in other phases of denominational work; promotion of

Evangelism and finally greater emphasis and effort in the department of church school enrollment and attendance. All the objectives were not reached during the specified time, but the results were gratifying to the Methodist leaders. The Crusade office reported that 3,948 recruits for the ministry and 9,293 additional recruits for other full-time phases of Christian service were enrolled. Over 150 thousand tithers and approximately a half million proportionate givers were recorded. Statistician Hoover of the Methodist Church reported that there was an increase in giving for all purposes during the Year of Stewardship of approximately $10,000,000.

E. *The Program of Progress of the Southern Presbyterians*

During the post-war period The Presbyterian Church in the United States, otherwise known as the Southern Presbyterian Church, promoted the *Presbyterian Program of Progress*. This was a five year campaign with several purposes including the raising of some $7,500,000 for capital funds. The campaign did not go over the top but around $6,000,000 was raised.

CHAPTER XIII

RECENT STEWARDSHIP DEVELOPMENTS

THE PURPOSE of this chapter is to bring up to date the history of the stewardship agencies and plans previously referred to in this book.

I. STEWARDSHIP AGENCIES

A. The Layman Tithing Foundation

The Layman Tithing Foundation is a non-profit corporation which was founded by the Methodist layman Thomas Kane in 1876 for the production of tithing literature and for the promotion of tithing. It was through this agency that Kane pioneered in promoting the Biblical doctrine of the tithe when it was all but unknown to American Christians. The aim of the foundation, as stated in its literature is to "make Stewardship literature available to all who seek to promote the Scriptural basis of giving." The foundation reports the annual distribution of nearly 2,000,000 pieces of literature to churches of all denominations. A Board of Directors composed of individuals from the various denominations, serve without remuneration, their only compensation being the satisfaction which comes from "helping Christians bear more fruit."

The foundation has literature available including 67 four-page tithing bulletins, and 81 different one and two page pamphlets and leaflets. The present address of this agency is: The Layman Tithing Foundation, 8 South Dearborn St., Chicago 3, Ill.

B. The Joint Department of Stewardship and Benevolence

The Joint Department of Stewardship and Benevolence is part of the National Council of Churches of Christ in America, having grown out of the United Stewardship Council, an interdenominational organization which from 1920 through 1950 maintained headquarters in Hillsdale, Michigan.

During the years above mentioned the United Stewardship Council rendered valuable service by promoting stewardship conferences in which officials of the various denominations met together to determine the best methods of stewardship promotion. Papers prepared and read by the leading stewardship officials for these conferences were usually published.

Through the years the United Stewardship Council published many pamphlets and books. Yearly bibliographies concerning the best stewardship books were also published by the organization for free distribution. It also pioneered in the use of audio visual aids for the promotion of stewardship. For ten years the weekly program *The Voice of Stewardship* was broadcast over the facilities of the ABC network.

One of the finest contributions of the Council was the gathering of the annual stewardship statistics from the various co-operating denominations. These statistics were compiled yearly and given wide publicity in both the religious and secular press. Membership for each denomination was recorded and the amounts given for benevolences, congregational expenses, and the total for all purposes were tabulated by each co-operating religious body for the preceding year. For the sake of comparison, the amounts were also broken down into per capita gifts for benevolence, congregational expenses, and total giving. By means of this information it was possible to chart the trends in giving in the denominations.

From 1921 through 1950 the secretary of the United Stewardship Council was Dr. Harry S. Myers, who carried the primary responsibility for promoting the varied phases of the work of the Council.

When on January 1, 1951 the *Joint Department of Stewardship and Benevolence* of the National Council of the Churches of Christ in America was organized the United Stewardship Council merged with the new organization. The work that was formerly carried on by the Council was taken over by the Joint Department. At that time, Dr. Harry S. Myers, the secretary of the Council was elected recording secretary for the Joint Department and shortly thereafter the Rev. Thomas K. Thompson, a Congregational minister who received his Master's Degree from Union Theological Seminary of New York City, became the executive director.

Thompson became known as a national leader in the field of stewardship through his position as secretary on the staff of the Missions Council of the Congregational Christian Churches. He was also elected to the chairmanship of the Visual Aids Committee of the United Stewardship Council, which office he held for three years.

Since assuming his office as the executive director of the Joint Department of Stewardship and Benevolence, Thompson has placed special emphasis on the tithe as the acknowledgment of God's ownership. He feels that "man's dominion over creation tempts him to consider himself God" and in his opinion the commonest form of idolatry in the history of mankind is "mammon-worship."

The Christian is called of God to be a steward, which means a manager, trustee or partner, Thompson declares, and "a steward has real freedom to use or abuse property." He points out that freedom is dangerous because men and nations often misuse their freedom to their own destruction.

One of the "mysteries" of Christianity is God's grace in committing to us weak, earthen vessels the carrying of the story of His love to a dying world when the Angel Gabriel, or some other heavenly messenger, could do the task.

"Our calling as stewards," says Thompson, "is to bring men to Christian handling of their time and money: To tell the story of God's love in giving Jesus Christ."

Personal contacts provide the Christian with an opportunity to witness regarding his faith and beyond this he can witness "in the giving of himself in his money which is his time and skill and Christian conviction in exchangeable form," concludes the writer.

With the organization of the Joint Department of Stewardship and Benevolence, the work formerly done by the United Stewardship Council and the United Church Canvass was combined and is now carried on by the above agency.

Reporting to the fourth annual assembly of the Joint Department of Stewardship and Benevolence meeting in Boston, Massachusetts, Thompson restated that the primary purpose of the organization is to serve as "a clearing house between the denominations to share techniques, plans and emphases," with semiannual meetings held to carry on the work.

Thompson points out a secondary purpose of the Joint Department, namely: "to help fund raisers of church related institutions."

Another means of promoting stewardship is the Joint Department's publication of an annual magazine called *Stewardship Facts* of which the May 15, 1955 circulation was 6,100 copies. A bibliography of the best books available on stewardship is also published biennially. *Statistics of Giving* is another publication of the Joint Department which contains vital facts with regard to Protestant giving through their denominations in the United States and Canada. November, 1954, issue of the *Statistics of Giving* showed that the denominations reporting to the Joint Department for the year 1953 gave a total of $1,537,132,309.

The Joint Department of Stewardship and Benevolence reported the following headline events as having taken place during the year 1954: One hundred and ninety-four representatives of church-related institutions attended the workshop on *Wills, Annuities, and Special* at Buck Hill Falls, Pennsylvania, November 2-4. Roy L. Smith rewrote the International Sunday School Lesson notes which the Joint Department has published in a book called *Stewardship Studies.* Fifty-five pieces of the best stewardship literature published in the United States were mailed to two hundred sixty stewardship leaders throughout the world.

In the winter of 1955 an intensive Seminar on Bequests for church board officials was conducted by the Joint Department. For 1956 the theme selected for nationwide emphasis in American Protestant circles was "remember your church in your will."

II. STEWARDSHIP PLANS

A. The Storehouse Tithing Plan

It was the promotion of the Storehouse Tithing Plan that made tithing meaningful to the people of Wesley Chapel in Cincinnati, Ohio, and also to the membership of the Geneva Methodist Church in New York State.

Though the plan at present is being promoted by no official person or organization, its vitality is seen in that it is still being used in adapted form in many churches. One such example is the Highland Park Baptist Church in Chattanooga, Tennessee.

In the autumn of 1950 the author of this volume, a member of the above church, was present as an eyewitness of stewardship history in the making, when Dr. Lee Roberson, the pastor of the great Highland Park Baptist Church, led his people in an enlistment campaign for tithers which resulted in 1800 members of the church signing the tither's covenant promising to "accept God's plan of giving and . . . bring a tithe (one-tenth) of . . . (their) income to the Lord's house each Lord's day during the coming year." In the succeeding years the number of tithers in this church has grown to over two thousand.

Here is the story of how the campaign was conducted. In the Highland Park Baptist Church, as is true with other Baptist Churches in the South, the fiscal year begins October 1.

In preparation for the inauguration of the campaign to enlist tithers, Dr. Lee Roberson first signed an acceptance card for himself and led the members of his family in doing the same. He next met with the board of deacons showing how important it was that they and their families lead the way. The result was that within a few days the forty-six deacons signed up 100 per cent.

With this kind of co-operation behind him the pastor next talked to his three hundred Sunday School teachers and officers during their regular weekly meeting held just before the mid-week prayer meeting, preceding the last Sunday of the month. Most of the teachers and officers signed up on the spot. Some took the cards home to think about the matter until Sunday.

The teachers and officers were then urged to present the matter of tithing in their Sunday School classes (beginning with the Junior department). They were also given directions concerning the securing of signed pledges from the church members in their classes. A report from the Sunday School was to be ready for the morning worship service showing how many had signed.

On Sunday morning the department superintendents were alert to see that the teachers followed through in the tithing enlistment program in their classes.

The pastor announced that he would speak on the subject, *The Golden Key* the last Sunday in September. To add interest to the occasion, just prior to the offering time two Junior boys came into the auditorium carrying a large golden key. The golden key was placed in a conspicuous place in front of the pulpit. The heads of the various Sunday School departments and organized Bible classes than came foward depositing *tithing acceptance cards* on a small table placed near the pulpit for the occasion. The number of tithers enlisted through the Sunday School was then announced.

The pastor's morning message on the subject *The Golden Key,* emphasized especially the spiritual prosperity that tithing brings. Following the invitation for accepting Christ and coming into the church, the *Golden Key Tithing Acceptance Cards* were quickly handed out to the audience of 3,000. The card reads as follows:

TITHING IS THE GOLDEN KEY

ACCEPTANCE CARD

I accept God's plan of giving and will bring a tithe (one-tenth)
of my income to the Lord's house each Lord's day
during the coming year.

*"Bring ye all the tithes into the storehouse, that there may be meat in mine
house, and prove me now herewith, saith the Lord of hosts, if I will not open
you the windows of heaven, and pour you out a blessing, that there shall not
be room enough to receive it.*

*"And I will rebuke the devourer for your sakes, and he shall not destroy the
fruits of your ground; neither shall your vine cast her fruit before the time
in the field, saith the Lord of hosts."*   Malachi 3:10, 11.

GOD HAS A PLAN FOR EVERYTHING!
ACCEPT HIS PLAN AND HIS PROMISE IS YOURS

Name ....

Address ....
"God loveth a cheerful giver"

Explaining that God's only method of finance is the tithe, and
that the deacons, who first signed the cards themselves, had voted
to adopt this Scriptural method for the church during the coming
year, and that the Sunday School teachers and officers had done
the same, the pastor appealed to the three thousand members
of his morning congregation to fall in line. The appeal was
continued in the evening service and in the mid-week prayer
meeting and also mentioned in connection with the services of
the first Sunday of the new church year in October.

In this enlistment campaign some 1800 members signed Acceptance Cards indicating that for the coming year they would accept
God's method of finance and bring the tithe to the Lord's house
every Sunday.

In the enlistment in the fall of 1953 some 2000 members of
the church signed Tithe Acceptance Cards. Though a continuous
program of visitation evangelism is carried on, not every member
canvass is conducted to secure pledges for certain amounts. Each
member receives a box of church envelopes which he is urged to
pick up in the church vestibule on the last Sunday of the old
church year. The envelopes that are not picked up after the first
Sunday of the new church year are mailed to the members.

Other than the tithe no one is asked to sign a pledge. No
financial statements are mailed to the members unless they so
request.

Though the pastor rarely devotes an entire message to the subject of tithing, he keeps the matter before his people each Sunday in brief two to three minute talks on the various phases of tithing and giving and the challenging ministry and need of the church.

Through this method of continuous stewardship education, the Highland Park Baptist Church of Chattanooga, Tennessee, without a doubt has one of the largest groups of tithers of any church in the United States. As a result the money given for all purposes through the church has risen from $40,434 in 1943 to $357,871.86 in the year which closed September 30, 1954.

B. *The Lord's Acre Plan*

The Rev. Dumont Clarke informed the author that this movement (see pages 67F.) has had a "tremendous growth and each year one of the most pleasing things is the increasing use of the plan in the mission fields."

The 1954 Annual Report of the *Lord's Acre Plan* carries the headline, *The Lord's Acre Movement Grows — North — South — East — West.* This report contains news items from *Lord's Acre* projects in practically every state of the Union as well as Canada, Africa, British Honduras and the Philippines.

In the report Mr. Clarke has an article entitled, "The Supreme Use of the Lord's Acre Plan," in which he reveals that the practice of dedicating projects for cause of missions is steadily growing and that such is the "supreme use of the Lord's Acre Plan."

The plan has an "inherent summons to each one to be a sacrificial worker in the cause of Christ" and will increasingly aid the missionary enterprise.

Pastors in rural areas may receive literature and information concerning the plan by writing Rev. Dumont Clarke, Director of the Religious Department, Farmer's Federation, Asheville, North Carolina.

C. *The Belmont Plan*

This plan (see pages 71f) is still in use. Dr. J. G. Patton, executive Secretary of the General Council of the Presbyterian Church in the United States writes that the Belmont Covenant Plan continues to be used extensively in that denomination though it is no longer referred to as the Belmont Plan and wherever it has been used there has been great advance in giving with many people continuing to tithe regularly.

CHAPTER XIV

STEWARDSHIP IN THE LARGER DENOMINATIONS

THE PURPOSE of this and the following chapter is to set forth some of the recent developments revealing the present status of stewardship in the various denominations. In order to acquaint the reader somewhat with these denominations, a brief historical sketch of each is given along with a statement of present numerical strength.

To secure the material for these chapters the author conferred personally or by correspondence with the stewardship or financial officials of some forty denominations. Certain questions were asked, which generally were as follows: (1) When was stewardship first emphasized in your denomination? (2) What is the official name of the stewardship organization of your denomination? When was it organized? Who is its present head? (3) Is tithing emphasized in your denomination? (4) Who are the leading stewardship writers of your denomination? (5) Can you give any other facts of historical interest with regard to stewardship in your denomination?

A questionnaire of this kind was sent out in 1943 and a similar questionnaire in 1954. Replies were received from thirty of the forty denominational officials approached. Not all of the responses were complete. Samples of current stewardship literature were also requested and received. Thus the files of the author contain at least six hundred pamphlets and periodicals received in 1943 or in 1954. We are, therefore, able to present our findings concerning the status of stewardship in some 25 denominations. This information has been supplemented in some cases by historical data, gleaned from other sources not hitherto mentioned in this volume.

Accompanying the historical sketch of stewardship for the various church bodies is a graph, in most cases, based on the denominational statistics taken from the yearbook, and from *Statistics of Giving* previously published by The United Stewardship Council and since 1951 by the Joint Department of Stewardship and Benevolence.

Statistics before 1920 were taken from the denominational yearbooks and per capita figures were obtained by dividing the

91

membership into the various sums for the different years. The long statistical tables are not shown in this volume but can be seen in the source books mentioned above.

I. THE AMERICAN BAPTIST CONVENTION

Formerly known as The Northern Baptist Convention, this body of Baptist churches in Northern and Western states changed the name to *The American Baptist Convention* at the annual meeting in Boston, May 24, 1950. Although missionary organizational developments originated in 1814, the Convention was not formed until 1907. The statistics for the year ending April 30, 1953 show 6,578 churches and 1,564,210 members in the American Baptist Convention.

The Department of Stewardship was organized in 1908. Convention minutes for 1909 show that a Stewardship report was then given, which advocated designating of at least one-tenth as a Christian duty.

In the Report of the Committee of Organization presented by Dr. Clarence A. Barbour of New York to the Northern Baptist Convention at Indianapolis in 1922 we read a statement that the development of the stewardship idea was considered so important that the committee felt the Board of Promotion should continue efforts along that line.

The recommendation of the Committee of Organization was evidently heeded for a report was read to the Northern Baptist Convention assembled in Milwaukee, 1924, announcing creation of a department of Prayer and Stewardship with the duty of promoting "throughout the denomination within the territory of the Northern Baptist Convention the ideals and practice of prayer and stewardship as a means of deepening the religious life and of increasing the efficiency of the denomination in the advancement of the kingdom of God." Departmental reorganization caused this work to be entrusted to a committee on stewardship, which sought to carry on its work in the churches through the Baptist League of Christian Stewardship and its local chapters which in turn have co-operated with the Baptist Young People's Union of America, itself noted for carrying on a vigorous tithing campaign.

The 1924 report pointed out that the Northern Baptist Convention adopted certain principles of stewardship at its meeting in Indianapolis, which have been guiding principles; namely, that God is owner of all and that man is a steward who should administer all that he possesses as a sacred trust for which he must give account to God. This truth should be acknowledged by the contribution of a definite portion of one's time, energy and possessions to the service of God and faithfulness in stewardship is the only adequate manifestation of gratitude and devotion to the Lord Jesus Christ.

Progress in the quality and quantity of stewardship literature has been realized and growing interest on the part of the churches is seen, stated the report. In one year ten pieces of literature were prepared and about 897,000 copies furnished to the churches at their request. The Committee announced its plan to provide suitable material for every department of the church for the proper training in stewardship of persons in every age bracket.

The report also told of field workers who were giving their entire time to promoting tithing, church efficiency and other aspects of stewardship. Also there were stewardship lectures given to students in the theological schools and at least twenty additional church officers clinics were conducted, said the Committee.

Another device to stimulate interest in stewardship is the pastor's essay contest. An annual stewardship period, usually in October, is observed by a growing number of churches, concluded the report of the Committee of Organization.

The above information is interesting in that it gives us a good view of the wide and varied activities carried on in the promotion of stewardship during the New World Movement. A rich literature of tracts and pamphlets on stewardship was built up during that period and distributed freely to the churches.

Stewardship among American Baptists is now promoted through the Department of Missionary and Stewardship Education, 152 Madison Avenue, New York 16, N. Y. of which William J. Keech is presently the director.

Responding to the author's inquiry with regard to the present status of stewardship among American Baptists, Keech summed it up in three parts; first the World Mission Crusade, following the war, in which $16,000,000 was raised for rehabilitation of the denominations war torn work around the world; secondly, there was a major denominational emphasis on stewardship which served to focus the attention of the people on the subject and provide valuable educational benefits; thirdly, the launching of so-called Sector Plans, which involved the use of the every member canvass plan on a highly organized area basis and were program building campaigns related to the resources of the people.

The term "Sector Project" merely signifies a geographical area. A central location is chosen and churches within fifty miles are invited to send their pastor and five financial leaders. The five laymen become the General Committee and over the ten-week period attend five training sessions. In these sessions they are supplied with manuals, calendars, turn-over charts, training films and other aids. The denominational leaders of the project do not go into the local churches, on the ground that one of the aims of the sector project is to develop local leadership so that each church can conduct its own canvass.

The "Sector Plan" training sessions open with the budget building session which is of great importance. Each church committee sits as a group, and with help from the rostrum begins building a dream budget. The budget includes what the church would like to do for itself and for missions if it had all the money it could wisely spend. As the session continues the leaders show charts, posters and films to point out that although taxes and the cost of living in the United States have gone up a great deal, per capita income has increased even more. Giving to churches, however, has not kept pace with this increase. The theme of the evening is the premise that the money is there and it is up to the finance committees to go after it by challenging the people in terms of building a greater program for the Lord Jesus Christ in their church, community and around the world rather than mere money raising. The finance committee also has the task of drawing blueprints capable of arousing the enthusiasm of the church members.

The leading stewardship writers of the American Baptist Convention are F. A. Agar, Paul Conrad, W. C. Muncy, Jr., and Earle V. Pierce. Dr. Agar has written a half dozen books on the subject which will be found listed in the Bibliography. Dr. Conrad, former executive secretary of the department of Stewardship has written several pamphlets and two valuable booklets, *The Chief Steward in the Local Church* and *This Way to a Thriving Church*. Dr. Pierce, many years a pastor and one year president of the Convention, is best known for his splendid volume, entitled *The Supreme Beatitude*. This book embodies a series of stewardship messages delivered by Dr. Pierce in the Baptist seminaries of both the North and South, and before many Baptist convocations.

The accompanying graph, based on yearly denominational statistics, presents a bird's eye view of stewardship results in the giving of American Baptists from 1894 through 1954. Notice that the giving to benevolences came to a peak in 1922 when per capita gifts reached $6.67. The effect of the controversy which began to rage throughout the Convention beginning in 1922 is seen in the downward trend in benevolence giving.

While benevolence giving took a downward course the giving for congregational expenses and total contributions reached a great peak in 1927 when the per capita giving to congregational expenses rose to $20.27 and total contributions to $24.85.

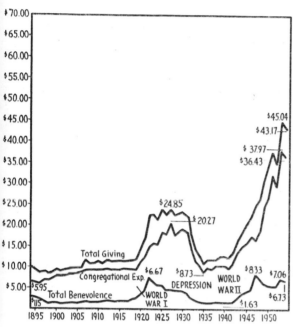

FIGURE 1. PER CAPITA GIVING IN THE AMERICAN BAPTIST CONVENTION (1894-1954) based on: (1) the statistics cited in **Survey of Fields and Work of The** Northern Baptist Convention (1894-1918), (2) the annual reports of the Convention (1914-1943), (3) the annual reports of the United Stewardship Council (1944-1950), (4) the annual reports of the Joint Department of Stewardship and Benevolence (1951-1954).

The effect of the depression is seen in the low levels of giving in 1935. The peak in benevolence giving was reached in 1947 when per capita giving was $8.33. The highest peaks of giving for congregational expenses and total contributions were reached in 1953 when per capita giving for congregational expenses rose to $37.97 and per capita giving for all purposes to $45.04.

II. THE SOUTHERN BAPTIST CONVENTION

In 1845 Southern Baptists withdrew from the General Missionary Convention, otherwise known as the Triennial Convention, and formed the Southern Baptist Convention, which was organized in Augusta, Georgia. The Foreign Mission Board and the Home Mission Board were both founded the same year. The Southern Baptist Convention in 1953 had 28,865 churches and 7,634,493 members.

Stewardship has been emphasized among Southern Baptists for many years, but increasingly so during the past twenty years.

In 1918 the *Seventy-Five Million Campaign* was launched and

Southern Baptists saw for the first time what could be done through concerted effort.

At the conclusion of the Seventy-Five Million Campaign, a Committee on Future Program was appointed. On May 13, 1925, in Memphis, M. E. Dodd brought the report of this committee, which called for: (1) Teamwork between state and Southern Baptist Agencies in financing objectives and allocations, (2) The incorporation of Every-Member Canvass in each church to make it possible for all members to have a part, (3) The recognition of the right of individuals and churches to designate their gifts if desired, (4) Following adoption of this report, the Future Program be known as the Co-operative Program of Southern Baptists.

In the Southern Baptist Convention the organization charged with the promotion of stewardship is the executive Committee with headquarters at 127 Ninth Avenue, North, Nashville 3, Tennessee. The Executive Secretary of the Committee in 1955 was Dr. Porter Routh and the Director of Promotion and Associate Secretary was Dr. Merrill D. Moore.

Stewardship is promoted in a very effective way through the Baptist Training Union Organization. Each year the month of November is set aside as Stewardship Month and during that month most of the articles in the Baptist Training Union Magazine deal with stewardship. In addition the lessons in the quarterlies for the various unions center around the thought of stewardship.

Stewardship is also promoted in the various components of the Training Union through their treasurers. A small pamphlet for use of the Senior B.Y.P.U. treasurer and Missionary Committee contains the following suggestions: (1) Lead the B.Y.P.U. to study the Bible Message of Stewardship and Missions. (2) Conduct Study Course in Stewardship. (3) Distribute leaflets on Stewardship and Missions. (4) Present plays on Stewardship and Missions. (5) See that every B.Y.P.U. member reads the Baptist Training Union Magazine, and the Journals of our Home and Foreign Mission Board. (6) Build up the Stewardship and Missions Section of the Church Library.

This tract is typical of those available for the treasurers and missionary committees in each age group of the Baptist Training Unions of the South.

When Southern Baptist Sunday Schools follow the recommendations of their denominational Sunday School Board, each organized class has a Stewardship Vice-President, one of whose duties is to "Urge Members To Make Tither's Pledge." Their conviction is that a "great deal may be accomplished toward developing the members in Scriptural giving by definitely promoting tithing in the class" until every member does so regularly.

In recent years the Executive Committee of the Southern Baptist Convention has given great emphasis to tithing. In 1947 the crusade to enlist *A Million Southern Baptist Tithers for Christ* was promulgated. In 1948 the slogan *Every Baptist A Tither* was popularized. In 1950 and the years following a *Tithers Enlistment Visitation* was promoted which involved personal visitation with the use of the *Tithers Enlistment Turnover Chart,* and this has continued through the years.

In 1953 The Southern Baptist Advance in Stewardship was inaugurated which brought the observation from Dr. Merrill D. Moore that Southern Baptists have made "remarkable progress" in teaching, training, evangelism, education, benevolence, missions and stewardship; but still have "only touched the hem of the garment."

The most urgent need, he declared, is in stewardship because here lies the means of supply in home and foreign mission fields, Christian education, hospitals, children's homes and state missions. Dr. Moore pointed out that the average per capita giving of Southern Baptists is "less than ten cents per week for missionary and benevolent causes, and less than sixty cents per week for all causes." These cold facts cause him to believe that there is "room for improvement."

Baptist leaders from twenty-two states and from the Southern Baptist Convention agencies have felt the urgency of the situation, says Dr. Moore, and prayed that the Lord would grant an unusual advance in stewardship. Leadership was provided in response to this prayer and study, they believe, as seen in the development of plans for Southern Baptist Advance in Stewardship in 1953, as adopted by the Southern Baptist Convention.

The central feature of this plan was *A School of Stewardship in Every Church,* October 18-25, 1953. The plans were promoted with enthusiasm and the hearty cooperation of every organization was evident, including state conventions, pastors and churches.

In the *Schools of Stewardship* the following texts were used: Adult, *Found Faithful,* Merrill D. Moore; Young People, *Good Stewards,* J. E. Dillard; Intermediate, *Partners With God,* Elizabeth Evans Terry; Junior, *The Talking Penny,* Bethann Van Ness. Sunday School and Training Union credits were given upon completion of the Adult or Young People's books and satisfaction of other requirements. Training Union credit was given for the completion of the Junior and Intermediate books.

A Leadership Rally was planned for each association in September to promote the School of Stewardship. A budget day was planned for each church and Pledge day and Every Member Canvass, usually for November 15 when subscriptions for the budget were taken.

The splendid success of the *Southern Baptist Advance in Stewardship 1953* is observed by Dr. Merrill D. Moore, who states that Southern Baptist Convention churches everywhere reported remarkable spiritual revivals, increased attendance and decisions for Christ, resulting in churches being strengthened and mission causes helped. "God opened the windows of heaven and poured out blessings," Moore testifies.

It is said that figures do not lie so let us turn our attention to the report of J. P. Edmunds, secretary of the Department of Survey, Statistics and Information of the Baptist Sunday School Board. Mr. Edmunds recorded the results of the *Advance in Stewardship 1953*. This report reveals that every state in Southern Baptist Convention territory showed higher giving for 1953 over 1952 with total gifts having increased 12.4 per cent and mission gifts 5.7 per cent. City churches led with an increase of 16.9 per cent and open-country churches had a 14.3 per cent increase.

The report also shows that in 1953 there were 804,374 tithers or a gain of 10.9 per cent over 1952. 6,374 churches had budgets of $10,000 or more and 989 churches had budgets of $50,000 or more.

Pastors were better provided for in 1953 with 4,007 churches paying a salary of $4,000 or more, of which number 295 paid a salary of at least $7,000. The report shows that in 1953 the average pastor's salary for churches with membership between 400 and 750 was $3,949; churches with membership between 1,000 and 1,500 averaged $5,383, and for those with membership between 2,000 and 2,999 the average was $6,978.

The Edmunds statement interprets the increased number of churches giving to missions as a reflection of the value of stewardship promotion, for figures show a jump from 26,565 to 27,388 in 1953, or a gain of 3.1 per cent.

Before we leave our study of the interesting statistics compiled by Edmunds, we call attention to a reminder that the work of stewardship training among Southern Baptists is not completed as yet, but only begun. Edmunds points out that the withheld tithe of Southern Baptists in 1953 could have built 22,366 church buildings costing $50,000 each or enabled the Foreign Mission Board to have multiplied their 1953 accomplishments by eighty-four. In home missionary endeavor this "withheld tithe" would have enabled Southern Baptists to establish new churches and erect accompanying buildings in more than 20,000 unchurched communities. The future attainments depend on stewardship emphasis and results, he concluded.

The Southern Baptist stewardship emphasis for the year 1954 was designated *Stewardship Revival 1954.*

Plan A (School of Stewardship)

This is the same plan which was used with such remarkable results in 1953. It was hoped that during 1954 the churches in each state not enlisted in Schools of Stewardship in 1953 would be reached with the same study and enlistment program used during the preceding year.

Plan B (Study, Sermon, Visitation)

This plan was recommended for churches that had already used the series of stewardship books. It was suggested that in the use of this plan four things be done: (1) Preach stewardship in five sermons Sunday through Wednesday; (2) Study *What the Bible Teaches About Stewardship,* using Bibles and Scripture references, for three nights; (3) Visit in Tithers Enlistment two nights; and (4) Use church organizations to promote attendance.

A recommended schedule for Plan B: (1) *Sunday* — Stewardship sermons in morning and evening services; stewardship lesson in the Sunday School and Training Union (as in the quarterlies on October 31). *Monday night* — Bible Study, 45 minutes, followed by sermon, with attendance promoted by Brotherhood and men of the church. (3) *Tuesday night* — Bible study, 45 minutes, followed by sermon, with attendance promoted by Training Union and Young people; a playlet by young people also possibly presented. (4) *Wednesday night* — Stewardship banquet (where convenient), Bible study, and sermon; attendance promoted by W.M.U. (5) *Thursday night* — Tithers Enlistment visitation, or visitation for high attendance on Sunday. (6) *Friday night* — Visitation as on Thursday. (7) *Sunday* — Victory Day. "Oversubscribe the increased budget in one day."

It was urged that the Stewardship Revival be held on or near October 31-November 7, 1954.

The Plan for 1955 — A One Night Stewardship Conference in Every Church between September 1 and October 15, 1955

The Southern Baptist Convention meeting in Houston, Texas, in 1953 adopted a recommendation that the state leaders consider the possibility of going into each church during 1955 with a special one night stewardship conference, utilizing leadership of the associations. Development of these conferences and plans

would involve consultation between state, associational and
church leaders. The suggestion of the resolution was to give
emphasis to "the Biblical message of stewardship, to explain
the Co-operative Program, and to give helpful suggestions on
financing the church and its program abroad."

The Plan For 1956 — World Missions Week

The Southern Baptist Convention meeting in St. Louis, June
2, 1954, adopted a recommendation that the Christian Stewardship Week in 1956 be referred to as *World Missions Week* with
encouragement for churches to "contribute to world missions
through the Co-operative Program," with the goal of increasing
the total undesignated budget receipts by 6 per cent annually.

*A Five Year Program Climaxing in 1964, One Hundred Fiftieth
    Anniversary of Triennial Convention*

The Executive Committee in December, 1953, approved a
recommendation calling for the Promotion Committee, in consultation with Southern Baptist Convention agencies, institutions and state secretaries among others to bring recommendations for a five-year program beginning in 1959 and climaxing
in 1964. The resolution also requested the Convention and its
Executive Committee to consider the advisability of celebrating
in 1964 the 150th anniversary of the founding of the Triennial
Convention.

A basic and underlying foundation of all that Southern Baptists are doing in the promotion of stewardship is *A Seven Step
Plan for Growing a Stewardship Church* as outlined by Dr.
Merrill D. Moore in a tract with this title. In introducing the
seven steps Moore states that God has a plan for meeting the
overwhelming needs of the world which involves His churches
and His people as set forth in the Scriptures in the doctrines of
evangelism, missions and stewardship. Since the progress of
God's plan depends upon stewardship, Dr. Moore emphasizes
that every church should be continually growing in the teaching
and practice of this plan and he sets forth seven simple steps
to do so, namely: (1) Teach Bible Stewardship, (2) Enlist Tithers,
(3) Plan Church Finances, (4) Increase Co-operative Program,
(5) Ask Every Member to Give, (6) Make Offerings Weekly,
(7) Handle Funds Well.

The accompanying graph is based on yearly denominational
statistics and presents a bird's-eye view of stewardship results
as seen in the giving of Southern Baptists from 1903 through
1954.

It will be noticed that the first peak in Southern Baptist
giving was reached in 1920, much earlier than in other denomi-

27874

nations. In that year Southern Baptists gave $4.39 per capita for benevolences, and total giving averaged $10.90.

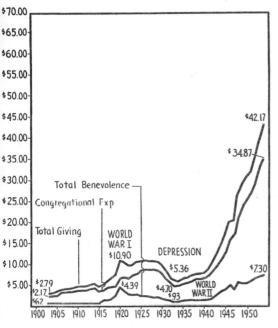

FIGURE 2. PER CAPITA GIV-ING IN THE SOUTHERN BAP-TIST CONVENTION (1903-1954) based on: (1) the annual reports of the Con-vention (1903-1927), (2) the annual reports of the United Stewardship Council (1928-1950), (3) the annu-al reports of the Joint Depart-ment of Stewardship and Be-nevolence (1951-1954).

During the depression Southern Baptist giving decreased greatly as will be seen by the graph, but the trend continued upward since that time. The highest peaks in Southern Baptist giving were reached in 1954 when $7.30 per capita was received for benevolences with a total average of $42.17 for all purposes. With the present strong program of emphasis on Tithers Enlist-ment, new heights in giving will undoubtedly be reached in the years ahead.

GIFTS TO MISSIONARY AND BENEVOLENT CAUSES

1936	1.	Methodist Episcopal, South	$ 7,283,233
	2.	Methodist Episcopal	7,191,714
	3.	Presbyterian, USA	6.423,210
	4.	Protestant Episcopal	4,844,194
	5.	SOUTHERN BAPTIST	4,624,515
1940	1.	The Methodist Church	10,596,950
	2.	Presbyterian, USA	7,268,240
	3.	SOUTHERN BAPTIST	6,267,263
	4.	Protestant Episcopal	4,017,198

1944	1. Methodist	17,000,336
	2. SOUTHERN BAPTIST	13,455,640
	3. Presbyterian, USA	8,865,837
	4. Protestant Episcopal	6,418,544
1948	1. Methodist	31,076,049
	2. SOUTHERN BAPTIST	28,472,014
	3. Presbyterian, USA	13,339,247
	4. American Baptist	11,967,080
1952	1. SOUTHERN BAPTIST	45,822,830
	2. Methodist	42,318,470
	3. Seventh Day Adventist	36,666,464
	4. Lutheran-Missouri Synod	23,883,173[1]
1953	1. SOUTHERN BAPTIST	48,427,760
	2. Methodist	46,882,218
	3. Seventh Day Adventist	39,137,675
	4. Presbyterian, USA	23,951,848[2]

[1] From a Report of the Associate Secretary and Director of Promotion compiled from *The Yearbook of American Churches* by Merrill D. Moore and furnished to the author for this study.

[2] Statistics for 1953 compiled from *Statistics of Giving* published November 1, 1954 by the Joint Department of Stewardship and Benevolence.

III. THE CONGREGATIONAL AND CHRISTIAN CHURCHES

Congregational churches date back to the Pilgrim Fathers and the colonists of New England in 1620. The Christian churches date back to the Wesleyan and revival movements at the end of the eighteenth century. These two groups were merged at Seattle in 1931. The denomination in 1953 had 5,597 churches and 1,269,466 members.

Stewardship has been stressed through the years in the promotional material. The First Congregational Church of Oak Park a few years ago published a leaflet giving the testimonies of tithers. The recent *History of Congregationalism* mentions "a Pilgrim Covenant of Stewardship" forming "a basis for nation-wide enrollment in proportionate giving" as having been proposed at the National Council in 1917.

At the present time the Congregational Christian Churches offer to their constituency thirty attractively written tracts and pamphlets on stewardship with emphasis on the tithe. One interesting project in which the denomination is engaged is the enrollment of 100,000 tithers in a *Fellowship of Tithers.*

Promotion of stewardship in the Congregational Christian Churches is directed by David H. Sandstrom, Executive Secretary of the Commission on Stewardship, 19 So. LaSalle St., Chicago, Ill.

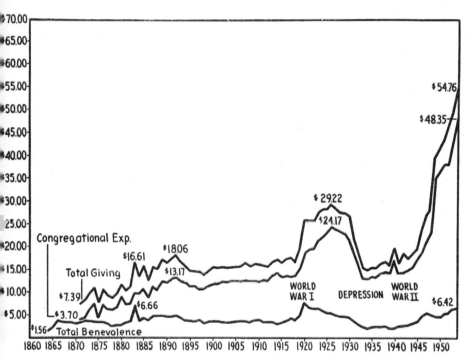

FIGURE 3. PER CAPITA GIVING IN THE CONGREGATIONAL CHRISTIAN CHURCH (1864-1954) based on: (1) the annual reports of the Congregational Church (1864-1931), (2) the annual reports of the United Stewardship Council (1932-1950), (3) the annual reports of the Joint Department of Stewardship and Benevolence (1951-1954).

The accompanying graph presents a bird's-eye view of stewardship results as seen in the giving of Congregational Christians from 1864 through 1954. The Congregational Christians reached their peak of giving for benevolences in 1920 as did the Southern Baptists. In 1920 the rate was $7.55 per capita for benevolences. Their first peaks in contributions to congregational expenses and total giving were reached in 1926 when $29.22 per capita for all purposes was achieved. The highest peak of giving was reached in 1954 when per capita giving for all purposes reached $54.76.

IV. DISCIPLES OF CHRIST

In the revival period of the early nineteenth century, a movement under Thomas Campbell and his son, Alexander, resulted in the establishment of a fellowship called Christians or Disciples. They emphasized Christian union, believing sects are unscriptural. Their mode of baptism is immersion. The 1953 statistics show that this denomination has 7,872 churches with 1,824,062 members.

During the early years the brotherhood known as the Disciples of Christ did not stress stewardship. The first major emphasis in a stewardship movement came during the Men and Millions Movement which carried on most of its activities during World War II.

After the war a real interest in tithing was shown as indicated by an article entitled "Putting the Stew in Stewardship," written by Secretary of Stewardship, Bert Wilson, which appeared in the *World Call,* official magazine of the Disciples of Christ.

Wilson humorously presented a sober fact when he stated that "the program of taking the oyster stew out of the church kitchen, and putting the Stew in Stewardship is now in full swing." He predicted extinction for the oyster.

The Stewardship Department ordered 50,000 each of four different tithing tracts from the Layman Company for free distribution to the churches which "took to this stewardship literature like flies to molasses."

During each of the past twenty-five years remarkable progress has been made in stewardship education. At the present time there are three periods of emphasis on stewardship during each year.

A. Stewardship Month

Stewardship month among the Disciples of Christ is generally observed in October, but may be placed in the program of the church when it will be most effective. During this period the attention of the church is focused on the following suggestions for its observance: (A) Preach stewardship sermons. (B) Use pageants, dramas, forums, short talks by laymen, oratorical contests, lantern slides, posters and other materials. (C) A school of stewardship for special groups, or elective courses for all youth and adult classes for the month. (D) Build stewardship worship programs in the church school. Reading contests and other educational projects could be carried forward. (E) Systematic distribution of stewardship literature, either through mail or through church services, or visitation campaign. (F) Climax the month with an opportunity to register any new enlistments. This should be a definite commitment in a consecration service.

B. *Stewardship and the Family*

The second stewardship emphasis of the Disciples of Christ relates directly to family as a vital unit in the church and the basic training unit in Christian living. Stewardship is set forth as the "heart of living" and giving a "definite part of the family program" for the family shares important things. Christianity is presented as a vital factor in all the decisions of the home in order to be effective in life. Christmas time or near Mother's Day is suggested as an appropriate time to consider such a program.

C. *Stewardship and Tithing*

The third stewardship emphasis during the church year of the Disciples of Christ relates to the presentation of the claims of proportionate giving through stewardship education with a definite period set aside for emphasis upon tithing as "a concrete expression of vital partnership with God." Recognition of God's ownership and man's stewardship should be taught. That taxes belong to our country is accepted and to acknowledge that God's kingdom is worthy of a proportion of one's income as "a vital safeguard against selfishness."

C. O. Hawley in 1943 made the statement that Disciples of Christ do emphasize tithing through a period from Easter to Pentecost set aside annually as a trial period. Literature is sent to the local churches advocating tithing in teaching and practice during this period, specifically the giving of 10 per cent of one's income to the work of the Lord.

Among the Disciples of Christ the responsibility for stewardship promotion and education is carried on through (1) Unified Promotion, (2) The Division of Christian Education of the United Christian Missionary Society, and (3) the State Missionary Society. The United Society previously carried the responsibility for stewardship but in 1935, when Unified Promotion was inaugurated, the task of stewardship promotion was allocated to this organization, and stewardship education is largely the responsibility of the Division of Christian Education of the United Society. The state societies help primarily in education and promotion of stewardship. C. O. Hawley is the Director of Unified Promotion.

The Disciples also have a National Stewardship Committee. In 1952 R. L. Thorp was called to be the National Director of Stewardship. His work is that of stewardship education and commitment rather than financial promotion which is carried on by others. He declares that their purpose and method is to "develop Christian stewards first which will result in a larger consecration of life and possessions."

During the years from 1946 to 1950 the Disciples engaged in *The Crusade for a Christian World of Disciples* which has been discussed in Chapter XII of this volume.

The period from 1954 to 1955 was set aside as *Our Year of Christian Stewardship,* for special emphasis on stewardship in the long range program of the Disciples of Christ.

At present the Department of Stewardship of the Disciples offers to its constituency some fifty pieces of literature including handbooks, wall posters, booklets and tracts. The Disciples under Thorp's leadership give a strong emphasis to tithing.

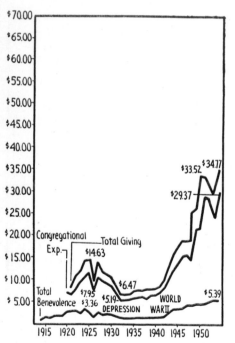

FIGURE 4. PER CAPITA GIVING BY THE DISCIPLES OF CHRIST (1914-1954) based on: (1) the annual reports of the Disciples of Christ (1914-1920), (2) the annual reports of the United States Stewardship Council (1921-1950), (3) the annual reports of the Joint Department of Stewardship and Benevolence (1951-1954).

The accompanying graph is based on the yearly statistics of the Disciples of Christ from 1914 through 1954. From it we notice that the highest point for benevolence was reached in 1954 when Disciples gave $5.39 per capita for benevolence while the per capita gifts for all purposes reached their greatest height in the same year of $34.77.

V. The Lutheran Church — Missouri Synod

This body, the largest constituent part of the Synodical Conference, was organized in 1838 and "holds an unwavering confessionalism and is a leader in the conservative group among the Lutherans." The 1953 edition of The Yearbook of American Churches lists the body as having 4,478 churches. *Statistics of Giving* published by the Joint Department of Stewardship and Benevolence lists the denomination as claiming 1,230,512 members in 1952.

The Evangelical Lutheran Synod in 1943 had no official stewardship department but the Rev. L. Meyer, Director of the Department of Missionary and Publicity, had charge of the promotion of such stewardship as was sponsored by the body.

Concerning the earliest Lutheran emphasis on stewardship, Meyer states that it has "always been the objective of our church leaders to stress 'stewardship' in all its implications." He explains that the history of the church made it necessary to stress the "stewardship" of money from the time of its organization in this country in 1838. People migrating here from Europe were not accustomed to giving money for the upkeep of the church because in Europe the church was subsidized by the State. Thus membership in a "free church" on American soil involved offerings for its operation.

Meyer adds that as the work of the church expanded the necessity for stressing giving became acute, resulting in the error of talking "money, money, money." In the past decade, he says, the stress has been on stewardship involving time, talents and possessions.

Concerning emphasis on tithing in the Evangelical Lutheran Synod, Meyer replied that he is not in a position to give any estimate as to the number of people who actually tithe in his denomination but that the average contributor gives approximately 5 or 6 per cent.

Meyer went on to call attention to the fact that they rely largely on the "indirect approach," seldom asking their people for money but operating on "the basis that when Christians are informed of the needs in the work of the Kingdom they will supply the wherewithal." This, he said, has been especially true in recent years. The depression forced very little retrenching and the denomination's present financial standing is "excellent," says Meyer. However, he admits that the increase in earning power of the Lutheran people "has not as yet reflected itself as it should have in their giving." He points to the time when they carried about a half million dollar debt, but indicates that for a number of years they have been balancing the budget without curtailment of the work, and appropriations made to their mission boards have in the past years usually exceeded their expenditures.

The Missouri Synod of the Lutheran Church has recently engaged in some reorganization which has affected the department charged with the promotion of stewardship. The mailing address is: Department of Stewardship Missionary Promotion, The Lutheran Church—Missouri Synod, 210 N. Broadway, St. Louis 2, Missouri.

In answer to the author's inquiry with regard to the present status of stewardship in the Missouri Synod, Assistant Counselor Rev. Waldo Werning replied that under the leadership of Pastor Herrmann the Lutheran church has been developing an "ongoing stewardship program" rather than featuring special stewardship campaigns. With this objective in mind, his department makes personal contacts with denominational leaders in various geographical areas of the church, and has also produced printed and audio-visual aids.

In recent years the Missouri Synod has been quite active in the promotion of stewardship, including material consisting of three sets of *Stewardship Forum Topics*. It also offers to its constituency eighteen attractive pamphlets such as *Radiant Living*, *Worshipful Giving*, and *What Is Proportionate Giving?*

The Synod also offers a fine selection of motion pictures with a stewardship emphasis, examples being: *All That I Have*, *Bringing Light*, *Another Door is Opened* and *Beyond Our Own Horizon*.

In addition filmstrips are available, such as *Why Do We Live*, *Guide for Living*, *Guide for Serving*, *Guide for Giving*. The motion pictures and the filmstrips can be ordered from Audio Visual Aids Department, 3558 South Jefferson Ave., St. Louis 18, Missouri.

The Missouri Synod furnished their pastors with literature to aid them in their leadership of the churches in stewardship. *Helps for the Pastor* is a booklet distributed by the Department of Stewardship Missionary Education and Promotion to the pastors of the Synod. Its entire 55 pages is filled with stewardship gems and sermon outlines as well as suggestions for the promotion of stewardship.

Another help for the pastor is *The Chief Steward*. This large, cloth bound book with bibliography was written by the Stewardship Counselor, the Rev. J. E. Herrmann, and speaks of the pastor's stewardship responsibility to his church. The Rev.

W. J. Werning, Assistant Stewardship Counselor, is the author of a 48-page booklet called *Partners with God*.

One of the significant events in the history of the Missouri Synod was the Okoboji Stewardship School held in 1952 at Camp Okoboji in Iowa. There plans were laid for district and circuit Stewardship Schools and suggestions made with regard to a stewardship program for local congregations. In preparation for the promotion of stewardship on these three levels several leaflets have been printed, such as *Manual for District, Circuit and Congregational Stewardship Committees*, a leaflet on *Stewardship Schools* (Circuit Level), another leaflet entitled *A Stewardship Program for the Local Congregation*, and one captioned *Parish Activities 1953-54*, in which a half dozen pages are devoted to the promotion of stewardship.

The accompanying graph which is based on the yearly statistics of the Lutheran Church-Missouri Synod presents a bird's-eye

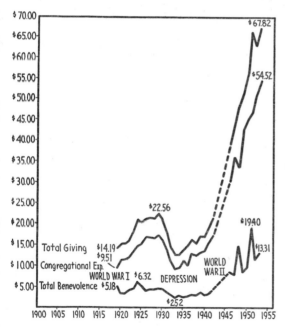

FIGURE 5. PER CAPITA GIVING IN THE LUTHERAN CHURCH (MISSOURI SYNOD) (1919-1954) based on: (1) the annual reports of the Missouri Synod (1919-1943), (2) no reports available to author (1944-1946), (3) the annual reports of the United Stewardship Council (4) the annual reports of the Joint Department of Stewardship and Benevolence (1951-1954).

view of stewardship results in this synod from 1919 through 1954. Notice how the total giving of the Missouri Synod soared to the high peak of $67.82 per capita in 1954, which is almost twice the per capita giving of the other large denominations. Of the larger denominations only the Southern Presbyterians surpassed this figure in the same year by reaching the high of

$75.54. Another remarkable record of this synod is in regard to gifts for benevolences which in 1952 reached $19.40 per capita.

VI. THE METHODIST CHURCH

The present organization of The Methodist Church is associated with the date May, 1939, when the unification of the three major branches of Methodism—The Methodist Episcopal Church; The Methodist Episcopal Church, South; and the Methodist Protestant Church, took place. These three uniting bodies were in unbroken historical connection with Methodism in America. The 1948 General Conference adopted a resolution stating that the Christmas Conference of 1784 is regarded as the date of the founding of the Methodist Church as an ecclesiastical organization. At that conference held in the Lovely Lane Chapel in Baltimore, Francis Asbury and Thomas Coke were elected superintendents and a program of expansion was outlined.

The Methodist movement began in England with John and Charles Wesley, leaders of an evangelical revival, and was carried to America in 1760 by Methodist emigrants from Ireland.

The 1953 edition of *The Yearbook of American Churches* shows that for the year closing December 31, 1952, The Methodist Church listed 39,906 churches and 9,180,428 members.

The Methodist Church has a great stewardship heritage. Though he may not have used the terminology, certainly John Wesley practiced stewardship, as all who are acquainted with the details of his life well know. It is evident that he preached stewardship of finances. For example, he observed in a message to his followers that some of the Methodists were twice as rich as before becoming Methodists; some fourfold as rich and some tenfold as rich. "Whilst you get all you can and save all you can, you do not give all you can," Wesley stated, "then you are tenfold more the child of hell than you were before."

One of the first stewardship statements of the Methodist Church was adopted at the General Conference of the Methodist Episcopal Church at Baltimore in 1908 when it adopted and placed in its dicipline a new paragraph headed *Tithing*. The statement affirmed that the evangelization of mankind requires "an adequate support of all the agencies used by the Church," and that to accomplish this purpose the "Scriptural doctrine of systematic giving should be taught in our pulpits and practiced by our ministers and members."

This statement suggests the influence of the Laymen's Missionary Movement which at that time was doing much to influence the churches toward systematic giving and missions.

The greatest stewardship movement in the Methodist Church was the Centenary Celebration. For this event the Methodist Episcopal Church and the Methodist Episcopal Church, South, united under the Joint Centenary Commission. Dr. Ralph S. Cushman, now Bishop of the Saint Paul Area of the Methodist Church, headed the Department of Stewardship during the Centenary Celebrations and led in a drive to secure a "Million Tithers in Methodism." It is reported that during this effort Dr. Cushman spoke at Columbus, Ohio and "persuaded 577 ministers and 247 laymen to enroll as tithing stewards."

The present attitude of The Methodist Church toward steward-ship endeavor can be seen in a statement of the General Conference as it is found in the 1940 edition of *The Doctrines and Discipline of the Methodist Church.* We therein read that the Methodist General Conference approves the Christian Steward-ship movement and calls for "effective co-operation" from every leader and organization within the denomination. The bishops who gave their approval of the movement were requested to contribute leadership to it in their respective areas.

The following areas and agencies were suggested as desirable for emphasis in the stewardship movement: "Jurisdictional, Annual, District, and quarterly Conference sessions; Summer Assemblies, Pastor's Schools, Standard Training Schools and Classes, Theological Schools, Christian Culture Institutes, Missionary Institutes, Laymen's Institutes, Laymen's Leagues, Steward's Leagues, Brotherhoods, Men's Clubs, Laymen's Group Meetings, Lay Programs in the Local Church, organized classes of the Church School, the use of pageantry, the distribution of pamphlet and leaflet literature, articles in the Church press, and effective preaching on stewardship from every pulpit of the entire church."

In addition, all the Methodist people were called on to pray that God would bless this effort of the church and that "sacrifice, and a new spiritual power will make Methodism a mighty force for redemption, righteous, and social justice to God's people everywhere."

The 1940 *Discipline* delegates the promotion of stewardship to the General Board of Lay Activities for the "cultivation and promotion of Christian Stewardship in the Methodist Church." It was specifically charged with initiating plans, developing literature and perfecting organization to accomplish this purpose.

The Executive Secretary of the General Board of Lay Activities located at 740 Rush St., Chicago 11, Illinois, has been Robert G. Mayfield, assisted by Associate Secretary E. Lamont Geissinger

and others. It was Mr. Geissinger who answered the author's inquiry about the present status of stewardship in The Methodist
Church, furnishing certain records and a bibliography of the
present stewardship publications.

On April 21, 1953 a *Quadrennium Program of Stewardship of
Possessions* was adopted by The Joint Stewardship Council of
the Methodist Church.

The fundamental principles suggested in this program include
Christian tithing to be presented as "an opportunity for pastors
and laymen;" a *"continuing process"* rather than a campaign,
with the key word being *"cultivation"* and the program voluntary. The emphasis was set forth as "Stewardship of Possessions"
with the tithe regarded as the "minimum standard of giving for
Methodist people" to be presented as *a means of grace* rather
than a legalistic procedure or a mere method of money raising.
The matter of computing the tithe and the manner of distributing it is classified as "a matter of individual conscience" and "a
covenant between the individual and his God." Regular channels
and exemplary leadership were stressed. The Quadrennium
Program also recommended the conducting of one-day Christian
Stewardship meetings and local church surveys to determine the
number of persons practicing tithing; four Sundays of stewardship preaching and teaching following sub-district stewardship
meetings; study courses on Christian Stewardship with emphasis
on tithing; and finally a second registration of tithers following
the month of preaching and teaching on the subject.

The above Quadrennium Program is underway and the monthly magazine called *The Methodist Layman* serves as a means of
promotion. The Methodist Church offers 17 pamphlets on Christian Stewardship, 15 on Christian Tithing, 9 on Church Administration and 5 on Plans for Stewardship Education.

The accompanying graph which has been worked out from the
yearly denominational statistics presents a bird's-eye view of
stewardship results as seen in the giving of Methodists from 1876
through 1954. By means of this graph we notice that Methodists
reached their highest peak of giving to benevolences in 1921
when they registered $6.23 per capita. In 1923 they reached their
first high peak of giving for all purposes with the record figure
of $24.78 per capita. The highest peak in total giving was reached
in 1954 with $37.53 per capita.

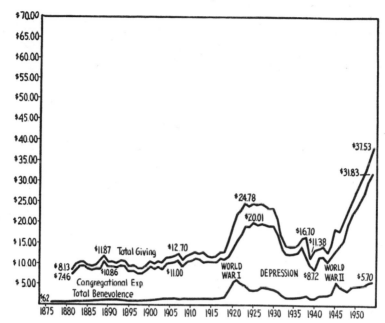

FIGURE 6. PER CAPITA GIVING IN THE METHO-DIST CHURCH (1876-1954) based on: (1) the annual reports of the Methodist Episcopal Church (1876-1939), (2) the annual reports of the United Stewardship Council (1940-1950), (3) the annual reports of the Joint Department of Stewardship and Benevolence (1951-1954).

VII. THE PRESBYTERIAN CHURCH IN THE UNITED STATES OF AMERICA

The Presbyterian Church in the United States of America is characterized by a representative form of government and Calvinistic theology. It appeared among the earliest colonists of America, the first church being established about 1640, and its first presbytery in 1706.

According to the 1953 edition of the *Yearbook of American Churches,* this denomination in the year closing December 31, 1953 had 8,390 churches with 2,441,933 members.

Stewardship has long been a part of the Presbyterian program. One of the oldest and best stewardship statements in existence was the one passed by the General Assembly of 1848. The stewardship movement in the Presbyterian Church reached great heights in the New Era Movement in 1921 when record achievements were realized in evangelism, missions, and giving.

The denomination has a Department of Stewardship in its Board of Christian Education which has its counterpart in the General Council's Every Member Canvass Department. The former provides the educational material and the latter promotes stewardship. The Rev. Arthur H. Limouze, D.D. was for many years the Secretary of Promotion of the General Council with the office being filled later by Dr. John T. Peters. The address is: Secretary of Stewardship and Promotion of the General Council of the Presbyterian Church U.S.A., 156 Fifth Ave., New York 10, N. Y.

The General Council of the Presbyterian Church is pioneering in what is known as *The Youth Budget Plan* whose purpose is to "develop young people in Christian character and service through participation in the financial support of the whole program of the church." The plan is flexible and adaptable to the needs of any church. According to the plan children and youth participate in raising a definite portion of the current expense and benevolent budgets of the church program, through personal pledges and systematic giving. The project is bolstered with an educational program conducted by a representative Youth Budget Plan Committee composed of children, young people and adults who are responsible to the session.

The number of churches adopting the plan has increased at the rate of approximately 14 per cent annually. The main object of the Youth Budget Plan is to teach stewardship to young people. In the execution of the plan committee meetings are held, budgets are made up, stewardship is studied and as a final effort the young people contact others their age to secure pledges for the program of the church.

The General Council also furnishes a splendid handbook entitled *Practical Stewardship Suggestions for the Pastor* which contains practical suggestions to help the pastor in the promotion of stewardship.

The Presbyterian Church in the United States of America engaged in a Stewardship Advance Program in 1955 for the purpose of raising a total of $18,000,000 of which $13,000,000 was designated for its basic program and $5,000,000 for an Advance Program to be used in connection with colleges, increased salaries and National and Foreign Missions.

The accompanying graph which was worked out from yearly denominational statistics presents a bird's-eye view of stewardship results in the giving of Northern Presbyterians from 1839 through 1954. Note the high peak of giving for all purposes attained in 1927 when contributions amount to $39.11 per capita.

Their highest peak in giving was reached in 1954 when the benevolence contributions reached $10.21 per capita and giving for all purposes reached $61.47 per capita. Southern Presbyterians the same year surpassed this figure with $75.54 per capita.

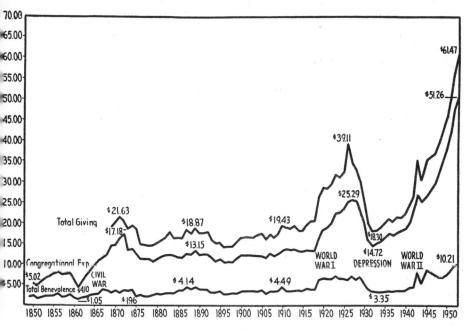

FIGURE 7. PER CAPITA GIVING IN THE PRESBYTERIAN CHURCH OF THE UNITED STATES OF AMERICA (NORTH) (1839-1954) based on: (1) the annual reports of the Presbyterian Church as cited from H. C. Weber, **Presbyterian Statistics Through One Hundred Years** (1839-1926), (2) the annual reports of the United Stewardship Council (1927-1950), (3) the annual reports of the Joint Department of Stewardship and Benevolence (1951-1954).

VIII. PRESBYTERIAN CHURCH IN THE UNITED STATES

The Presbyterian Church in the United States is the branch of the Presbyterian Church which separated from the main body at the time of the Civil War. It is often called the "Southern Presbyterian Church." The *Yearbook of American Churches* shows that in the year ending March 31, 1953, this denomination had 3,706 churches with 718,791 members. It has for several years made a splendid showing in giving to benevolences.

When the General Assembly of the Presbyterian Church of the United States was first organized as a separate body in 1861 that

Assembly adopted a statement declaring its missionary purpose and obedience to the Lord's last command, "Go ye into all the world, and preach the Gospel to every creature." This they regard as the "great end" of their organization and obedience to it the "indispensable condition of the Lord's promised presence."

The Southern Presbyterian Church has long emphasized the importance of sacrificial giving bolstered by the background of the sovereign ownership of God. However, the Southern Assembly began to move very definitely in the direction of a stewardship emphasis in 1911, when the first steps were taken to organize "The Committee on Systematic Beneficence." In the two or three years that followed, the work of this committee was crystallizing and the Assembly officially approved the Every Member Canvass plan. In 1915 about one-fourth of the churches were reportedly following the Every Member Canvass plan. The use of this plan increased so that by 1918 practically all the churches in the Southern Assembly were using it. This systematic approach to the members of the church is regarded as one of the most important factors in the increase of per capita giving during the period from 1916 to about 1924.

The official name of the Southern Assembly's department of stewardship is the *Committee on Stewardship and Finance,* Presbyterian Church in the United States. A manual was adopted in the 1932 General Assembly to serve as a guide for the work of the committee and was revised by the 1942 General Assembly. The manual enumerates the duties of the Committee on Stewardship and Finance which primarily is to encourage the promotion and practice of Stewardship throughout the denomination; to assemble, review and recommend to the General Assembly the annual budget of expenditures for the Executive Committees and other agencies of the Assembly and an Asking Budget for the ensuing fiscal year; to handle matters involving inter-committee co-operation, finance, education and promotion as well as recommend to the Assembly necessary adjustments in the plans and work of the committees or agencies of the Assembly and finally to supervise and direct the work of the Committee on promotion.

B. K. Tenney, Secretary of the Committee of Stewardship and Finance, attributed the splendid per capita benevolence giving for the past few years to a sustained effort along three lines, namely: teaching and practice of the principles of stewardship, including the sovereign ownership of God and accompanying stewardship of man together with setting aside one-tenth in acknowledgment of God's ownership and dedicating the remainder to God's will; the inculcation of understanding concerning the community and world-wide program of the church; and the development of denominational leaders in the stewardship field. Tenney commented that although they are among the leaders in per capita giving, they feel that standards of giving are to be compared not with others, but with God's blessing and the need of the world for Christ. In this light a sense of shame is felt that the giving is not larger, said Tenney.

Concerning the Belmont Tithing Plan, Tenney remarked that it is primarily for the purpose of introducing a congregation to tithing in which the members are asked to tithe for a limited period of time in connection with some special objective. Pastors are interested in adopting the tithing plan as a permanent practice and therefore are not using the plan as widely as once was the case.

The Executive Secretary of the General Council of the Presbyterian Church in the United States is the Rev. J. G. Patton, D.D. whose address is 341 C Ponce de Leon Ave., N.E., Atlanta 5, Georgia.

An article printed in *Stewardship Facts, 1953-54,* written by Dr. Patton, entitled: *A Year-Round Stewardship Program,* declares that "Stewardship is a manner of life and it cannot be set off into a segment of the church year." A year-round program is essential, says Dr. Patton, and a stewardship emphasis without such a program is doomed to failure. He also points out that an "inferior program that is worked is better than a superior program which is made and forgotten."

First on the essential list in a stewardship program is the appointment of a stewardship committee, says Patton, and the committee's first task is to analyze the stewardship opportunities as well as the obligations of the local churches and the giving abilities of the members. It is usually found that the church has not offered a program that will really challenge their people.

The financial setup of the local church is scrutinized, including all departments, for many churches have no system while others sometimes have practices which hinder rather than help the teaching of stewardship, claims Dr. Patton.

Based on such studies the committee is able to submit a program that will produce a stewardship minded church.

Patton lists seven elements in the Stewardship Program which we have summarized as follows: (1) *Stewardship Preaching*: Stewardship preaching throughout the year is an essential in the stewardship education of the church. (2) *Audio-Visual Aids*: The program will include frequent use of audio-visual aids.

These may be secured from denominational headquarters. (3) *Stewardship Emphasis*: This committee should encourage the teaching of stewardship in the various departments of the church. (4) *Stewardship Study Classes*: Special stewardship study classes should be arranged annually or every other year for the development and the training of stewards. (5) *Stewardship Literature*: The proper use of stewardship literature has been found essential by every church that has developed a stewardship program. Never has this literature been so abundant and so attractive, and it may be obtained free of charge from denomination headquaters. (6) *The "Separated Portion"*: We believe that no stewardship program will develop true stewards unless in this program the "separated portion," beginning with the tithe, is stressed. Such an emphasis should be the heart of every stewardship approach. (7) *The Every Member Canvass*: The stewardship program has at its focal point the season of the Every Member Canvass. If there has been proper training throughout the year and proper preparation for the canvass, it should prove to be a time of high spiritual experience.

Patton concludes the article by warning against "hit-and-miss" methods. A plan backed by prayer and labor will result in the developing of a spiritual life in the congregation and eliminate the irritating financial problems which should have no place in church life, asserts Patton.

One of the 36 attractive pieces of literature put out by Southern Presbyterians is a bulletin which asks the question, "Why Tithe?" and answers it with the following outline:

I. The Tithe Is God's Plan
   A. It Is Biblical (Lev. 27:30)
   B. It Acknowledges God as Sovereign Owner (Mal. 3:8)
   C. It is evidence of Consecration (II Chron. 31:6)
   D. It is a Beginning Point in Sharing (Duet. 12:6)

II. Christ Confirms the Tithe (Matt. 23:23)

III. Christ Practiced the Tithe
He would not have failed to obey a commandment he told others to obey. His enemies, continually seeking opportunities to bring accusations against Him, never brought the charge of failing to tithe.

IV. God Blesses the Tithe
   A. By giving us a sense of being in the will of God.
   B. By giving us a new power in prayer. "Prove me," says God.
   C. By taking the sting out of giving. (Once the tithe is set apart, the question of giving is settled).

D. By giving us a testimony men can understand.

E. By providing amply for the financial needs of God's work.

F. By giving us material blessing — not a guarantee of wealth but enough to meet our needs.

The message of the bulletin is brought to a close by promising seven surprises to the person who begins to tithe. You will be surprised, it states, at . . .

1. The amount of money you have for the Lord's work.

2. The deepening of your own spiritual life.

3. The ease with which you meet your obligations.

4. The pleasure you will find in larger giving.

5. The soul satisfaction in practicing stewardship of time, talents and possessions.

6. A new appreciation of the goodness of God.

7. Yourself . . . for not adopting the plan sooner.

The accompanying graph which has been worked out from the yearly denominational statistics presents a bird's-eye view of stewardship results as seen in the giving of Southern Presbyterians from 1889 through 1954. Notice that in 1922 Southern Presby-

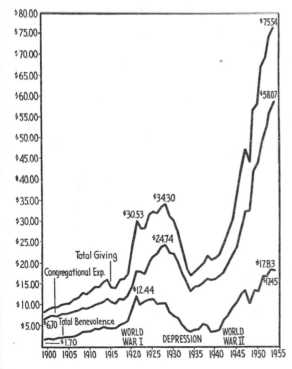

FIGURE 8. PER CAPITA GIVING IN THE PRESBYTERIAN CHURCH OF THE UNITED STATES (SOUTH) (1898-1954) based on: (1) the annual reports of the Presbyterian Church in the United States as cited from a statistical study of the Committee of Finance and Stewardship and from H. C. Weber, **Presbyterian Statistics Through One Hundred Years** (1898-1926), (2) the annual reports of the United Stewardship Council (1927-1950), (3) the annual reports of the Joint Department of Stewardship and Benevolence (1951-1954).

terians reached a high peak in benevolence giving of $12.44 per capita and in 1928 a high for all purposes of $34.30 per capita. However, this latter figure was more than doubled in 1954 when the denomination reported an all time high of $75.54 per capita in total giving. Thus Southern Presbyterians have the honor of leading all of the larger denominations in per capita giving for all purposes. The Lutheran Church — Missouri Synod is a close second having given $67.82 per capita for all purposes in 1954.

IX. PROTESTANT EPISCOPAL CHURCH

This body, a descendant of the Church of England, entered the colonies with the earliest settlers at Jamestown in 1607. The Protestant Episcopal Church became autonomous and adopted its present name in 1789. The statistics submitted to the Joint Department of Stewardship and Benevolence for the year ending December 31, 1952, show a membership of 1,690,000 persons.

The Rev. Howard V. Harper, Executive Director of The Presiding Committee on Layman's Work informed the author that the Episcopal Church has been recently engaged in the teaching of the concept of stewardship. The Diocese of Michigan reports considerable success in the promotion of tithing.

The Layman Tithing Foundation of Chicago published a leaflet by Bishop Richard M. Emerich, of the Episcopal Diocese of Michigan, which consists of a summary of one of his addresses entitled *Nine Reasons for Modern Tithing*. A summary of the reasons mentioned therein is as follows: a method of intelligent giving; freeing church leaders from preoccupation with money; rich or poor alike are on an equal footing before God; the church to speak in a dignified manner about responsibility rather than stooping to begging; everyday gratitude to God for His many gifts; giving a fixed percent of one's income teaches responsiblity in the handling of possessions; provides the satisfaction of having an honest and important participation in God's work in the world; has Scriptural authority; and finally helps one to see that all phases of life, even a person's budget, can bring glory to God.

The man who doubtless is the outstanding stewardship writer of the Protestant Episcopal Church is The Rev. Clarence R. Hayden, Jr. who has authored at least five attractive booklets: the *All That I Am Series* in which the author deals with *My Time, My Talents, My Treasure* and two others entitled, *Of Thine Own* and *As The Lord Has Blessed You*. These well written treatises deserve the widest circulation, and may be ordered from The Presiding Bishop's Committee on Layman's Work, 281 Fourth Ave., New York 10, N. Y.

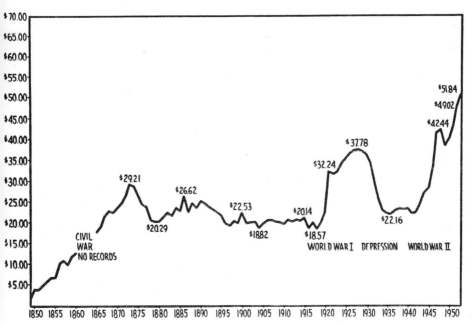

FIGURE 9. PER CAPITA GIVING IN THE PROSTESTANT EPISCOPAL CHURCH (1849-1954) for all purposes based on: (1) the annual reports of the Protestant Episcopal Church as cited in **The Living Church Annual** in 1940 (1849-1940), (2) the annual reports of the United Stewardship Council (1941-1950), (3) the annual reports of the Joint Department of Stewardship and Benevolence (1951-1954).

In one of these booklets Hayden comments on a recent report of the Joint Department of Stewardship and Benevolence dealing with the giving of church members in the year 1951. He observes that per member gifts of the Episcopal Church amounted to $33 for total congregational expenses and $6.34 for benevolences which included $1.23 for foreign missions; making a total of $39.34 per capita annually or seventy-five cents per week. Tithing would have brought in $158.40. In spite of increased giving, less than two cents out of each dollar is contributed for religious welfare and educational purposes that depend on such support. Giving is not keeping pace with increased incomes, charges Hayden.

X. UNITED LUTHERAN CHURCH IN AMERICA

The United Lutheran Church in America dates back to the Ministerium of Pennsylvania, organized in 1748, and beyond that to early colonial days. It represents the union of the General Synod, the General Council and the United Synod of the South in 1918. The report turned in to the Joint Department of Stewardship and Benevolence for the year 1952 shows a membership of 1,399,078.

A. The History of the Lutheran Layman's Movement for Stewardship

The body which is charged with responsibility for the promotion of stewardship in the United Lutheran Church in America is the Lutheran Layman's Movement for Stewardship. A brief history of this movement is helpful to our understanding of the denomination's stewardship emphasis.

When the General Synod, the General Council, and the United Synod in the South were merged in 1918 into the United Lutheran Church in America, the phrase "stewardship and benevolence" was already in common use, especially in the General Synod. It was introduced into the congregations by the Layman's Missionary Movement which had already been functioning for eleven years, having been organized in 1907 in Sunbury, Pennsylvania.

The original objective of the Layman's Missionary Movement was to devise ways and means to increase freewill offerings for benevolences in all General Synod congregations. The method selected for this purpose was the Every Member Visitation with aids such as the budget, duplex envelopes, pledge cards, and quarterly statements. When the merger came the Layman's Missionary Movement was considered of sufficient importance to be taken over by the new United Lutheran Church in America and made the official agency for the extension of its program to all the congregations included in the merger.

By 1920 the stewardship idea had made such headway among the leaders of the United Lutheran Church in America that it approved a proposal for the establishment of a Department of Stewardship. However, because the Layman's Movement was considered the best agency for stewardship promotion the resolution did not pass.

The constitution of the Layman's Movement purposes the dissemination through proper channels of "a true Biblical conception of the stewardship of life and possessions," as well as "stimulating a sense of responsibility on the part of the members toward supporting the work of the Church." Introducing approved methods of securing benevolence and conducting the annual Every Member Canvass are also set forth as the agency's duties.

This constitution was approved by the Buffalo convention thus placing the United Lutheran Church squarely back of a Christian Stewardship program.

In the Chicago convention, 1924, the foundation was laid for the activities of the Laymen's Movement for the following years in fields of student aid, Every Member Canvass, use of the Duplex-Envelope, in the seminaries, summer schools and applied stewardship. The Chicago Convention, upon recommendation of the Layman's report, also set aside the month of November of each year as stewardship month. The Chicago Convention also approved a recommendation sponsored by the Laymen's Movement calling for pastors to emphasize stewardship during November through sermons, Sunday School classes, young people's organizations, women's organizations, the Brotherhood and through the distribution of literature. The convention also requested various departments of the church to insert suggestions for stewardship studies in their programs.

B. *Secretary Arthur P. Black Reports on Stewardship Results in 1938*

Reporting to his denomination through *The Lutheran,* Arthur P. Black, the dynamic secretary of the Lutheran Laymen's Movement for Stewardship, listed several results of the efforts of his organization, including official recognition of Christian stewardship fundamentals from nearly all the 31 synods, over 100 conferences and more than 3,900 congregations. An additional one thousand pastors, or four out of every five, ordered Every Member Visitation and stewardship literature. One hundred and seventy men were added to the United Lutheran ministry through the student aid program of the movement.

Nearly sixteen million pieces of stewardship and Every Member Visitation literature were printed and distributed free of charge by the Laymen's Movement since 1930. Preparation of stewardship messages in cooperation with Lutheran officials was carried on since 1937.

Denominational periodicals such as, *The Lutheran, Lutheran Men, Augsburg Teacher, The Parish School Magazine, Luther League Review*, devoted increased space to stewardship matters. A circulating library was operated by mail to make good stewardship available to pastors and interested laymen.

As a result of all the above effort stewardship is presented from more pulpits, Sunday School classes, summer schools, Brotherhood programs, seminaries, boards and agencies than ever before and the list is growing.

C. The Status of Stewardship in the United Lutheran Church (1943)

In answering the question as to whether tithing is emphasized in his denomination, Black replied in the negative. The principle is approved by the Laymen's Movement but has never been pushed to any great extent. "We 'play up' the tithing programs of our pastors from time to time," added Black. A folder enjoying wide circulation in United Lutheran circles is entitled: *When Pastors Talk Out Loud on Tithing Things Happen.*

Black mentioned the Rev. P. D. Brown, D.D., pastor of the John's Lutheran Church in Salisbury, N.C., and the Rev. Carl H. Bartsch, pastor of Trinity Lutheran Church, Minneapolis, Minn., as outstanding examples of men who preach and promote tithing with great success in the United Lutheran denomination.

The Rev. Dr. Walton H. Greever, Secretary of the United Lutheran Church in America, and author of the book *The Work of the Lord,* provides classic stewardship material in chapter six of the volume. George Louis Rinkliff was also named by Black as a leading stewardship writer. Black reports that twenty-nine of the thirty-two synods of the U.L.C.A. have committees on stewardship.

Freewill offerings for benevolences which have increased each year for nearly a decade is a sign of stewardship growth in the U.L.C.A., Black feels. However, he wrote, "we are not scratching the surface, as a church. Many of our pastors are digging deep, and getting wonderful results. But many others continue to be self-centered rather than Christ-centered, so are doing nothing in the field of stewardship worthy of the name."

The Secretary of Stewardship in the United Lutheran Church in 1955 was Henry Endress with headquarters at 231 Madison Ave., New York City, and head of the Lutheran Laymen's Movement for Stewardship was Paul I. Folkener of Baltimore, Maryland. Folkener personally testifies to the blessing that tithing has brought to him and his family.

The accompanying graph which has been worked out from the yearly denominational statistics throws interesting light on the stewardship story of the United Lutheran Church as it has manifested itself in giving. The United Lutheran Church reached a high peak of giving for all purposes in 1926 when the per capita gifts were $24.25. A high peak in benevolence giving was reached in 1928 when the church registered $5.20 per capita. Its lowest point in giving for all purposes was $12.55 per capita in 1933. A low point in benevolence giving was $2.06 in 1935. Since that time the trend has been upward until the highest peak in giving for all purposes was reached in 1954 when United Lutherans gave $50.25 per capita.

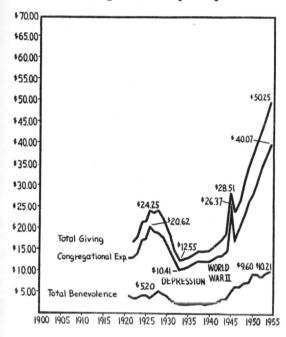

FIGURE 10. PER CAPITA GIVING IN THE UNITED LUTHERAN CHURCH IN AMERICA (1921-1954) based on: (1) the annual reports of the United Stewardship Council (1921-1950), (2) the annual reports of the Joint Department of Stewardship and Benevolence (1951-1954).

CHAPTER XV

STEWARDSHIP IN THE SMALLER
DENOMINATIONS

THE MATERIAL of this chapter is necessarily limited to the number of denominations reported and the amount of information regarding each. Inquiries were sent only to those smaller denominations known to maintain departments of stewardship or to have made a notable contribution in the field of stewardship. Not all replied. However, the fifteen denominations reported herein are among the smaller church bodies making significant contributions in the field of stewardship.

I. THE ASSEMBLIES OF GOD

The Assemblies of God is an evangelical, pentecostal body formed in Arkansas in 1914. In one their official statements, written by General Secretary J. Roswell Flower, and reprinted in booklet form, entitled: *The Origin and Development of the Assemblies of God,* we read that they believe in "the necessity of the new birth and the need of personal holiness," along with "the privilege of personal Baptism in the Holy Spirit with Pentecostal fullness," followed by the sign of "speaking in other tongues as the Holy Spirit gives utterance." The author states that approximately 90 per cent of the membership claim to have received this experience with the remainder firmly believing in it.

The document claims a high per cent of increase of churches and personnel annually. In September 1942 affiliated and co-operative churches numbered 4,840 with an enrolled membership of approximately 222,730. A recent list of ordained ministers include approximately 4,260 names in addition to 2,680 licentiates and exhorters. The Sunday School literature from the denomination's headquarters is sent to approximately 6,500 Sunday Schools with an enrollment of 500,000 students.

In proportion to its size this denomination does a remarkable volume of missionary work as will be seen from statistics reported by Flower. He states that 1942 ended with their having 362 missionaries and 1,231 native workers occupying 1,420 mission stations and out-stations on at least 40 mission fields. Missionary giving kept up with the increase in workers with 700 thousand dollars received for foreign work during the year 1942.

In a letter to the author, Flower discussed present status of stewardship in his denomination stating that the Assemblies of God were born in a revival atmosphere, and complete consecration, including tithing, was emphasized by all of their early pastors and evangelists. There is scarcely any literature on the subject and no department of stewardship, said Flower. However, the churches follow the tithing principle.

The independent assemblies were organized into a general fellowship in 1914, continued Flower, and a statement approving the principle of tithing for church support was adopted. A few articles and tracts have been written and published but are "fragmentary." Assemblies of God rely on "the revival spirit in the hearts of our people," explained Mr. Flower, and "no difficulty along financial lines" will be encountered.

II. BAPTIST GENERAL CONFERENCE OF AMERICA

This body was formerly known as the Swedish Baptist General Conference of America and has been in operation since 1879. Denominational headquarters are at 5750 N. Ashland Ave., Chicago 26, Ill. It reports 366 churches with 48,647 members.

In the *Reports of Committees* to the Baptist General Conference of America assembled in Jamestown, New York, a *Stewardship Committee* report was read under date of June 2, 1954, bearing the signature of its secretary, Clarence O. Swanson. During the two and one half years of the committee's existence the members "endeavored by various methods to help in acquainting the members of our churches with the great opportunities God has opened to our General Conference."

May, 1954, was designated Conference-wide *Stewardship Month* with the theme, "Lord, what wilt thou have me to do?" in relation to time, talents and treasure. Promotion was carried on by tracts, posters, bulletin covers, and articles in *The Standard*. May 12 was designated a day of prayer for the General Conference.

A special effort was made through the conference periodical to bring about "substantial increases for the many pastors who are so sadly underpaid."

The Standard, in November 1953, carried a reprint from the *Chicago Tribune* entitled, "Protestant Giving on the Increase," based on the yearly report *Statistics of Giving,* issued by the Joint Department of Stewardship and Benevolence. The editor called attention to the Baptist General Conference which reported $4,741,422.01 for local work, benevolence and missions during the year 1952-1953 which averaged $92.86 per member. About one fourth of the total, over $23.00 per member, went to missionary endeavor, said the editorial. Prof. Alphin Conrad, a recent stewardship writer of the Baptist General Conference, wrote a manuscript entitled *The Divine Economy* which was published in 1954. Conrad's book sets forth the theological basis of stewardship. The major premise is that God has placed His power and resources under the law of stewardship for the initiation and fufillment of His purpose in the world. The author states that God's purpose has been projected through the Son and the Holy Spirit to the believer for partnership with Him in the completion of His program. The volume is designed for use as a textbook in colleges and seminaries.

III. BRETHREN — CHURCH OF THE BRETHREN

German pietists from Crefeld, Germany, under the leadership of Peter Becker, entered the colonies in 1719 and settled in Germantown and Philadelphia, Pa. They claim no other creed than the New Testament and hold to the principles of nonviolence, temperance and the expression of their Christianity through a good life. The denominational headquarters is at 22 South State St., Elgin, Ill. and in its report to the Joint Department of Stewardship and Benevolence for the year 1952 a membership of 168,258 was listed. The author was in correspondence with H. Spencer Minnich, financial secretary of the Church of the Brethren in 1943, and learned that the denomination has no official department of stewardship but regards stewardship as "inherent in the Christian gospel." Stewardship education is promoted "with emphasis on the stewardship principle in the Christian faith." This is done through their church periodicals, Church School lessons, pamphlets, slides, sermons and other channels. "Tithing is emphasized in our denomination," wrote Minnich, but "we do not make a dogma of it and do not insist on it."

J. Henry Long was later charged with the promotion of stewardship in the Church of the Brethren. He reported that the program of stewardship education was stepped up considerably since 1943. An Audio-Visual Department was established recently with the view of increasing the use of this means of communicating stewardship truths. Workshops and conferences for pastors, finance committees and other lay workers involving use of charts are increasing.

Special packets of stewardship materials relating to local church finances are being mailed to pastors and selected lay leaders. Emphasis upon the tithe as the minimum standard for Christian giving and the use of the every-member canvass is being encouraged along with a system of budgeting, and weekly offering envelopes with a stewardship message on each is being promoted, says Long. The 1948 Annual Conference authorized a *Brother-hood Fellowship of Tithers* and enrollment forms are available for adults, young people and children. Long feels that definite progress is being made in stewardship education and as evidence cites the 55 per cent increase in giving for all benevolences in 1953 as compared with the year 1947, as well as a 150 per cent increase for local needs in the same period.

There was an overall increase of 109 per cent in total giving for all purposes during those years. The per capita gain was over 100 per cent, the figure being $20.14 in 1947 and $40.36 in 1953. In spite of this gain, Long confessed that "we are woefully below the level of the tithe, but we are making progress."

The Church of the Brethren is promoting the Fellowship of Tithers and the names of the tithers in the denomination are listed in a booklet bearing the same title, with the exception of those who request their identification withheld.

The Church of the Brethren makes available to its constituency some thirty-three pieces of attractive literature on stewardship and tithing. An example is the folder by Harper S. Will entitled *Tithing Will Help You.* Five points are stressed therein, namely that tithing acknowledges God's ownership over all things; makes man a partner with God; makes the experience of God a reality; gives stability to the church; and makes resources available for extending the kingdom.

Long and Minnich have both devoted time in recent years to the preparation of literature dealing with "the stewardship of accumulated possessions," which discusses wills, annuities, bequests, etc. The Brethern regard it as "a great undeveloped field," and are pioneering in the effort of raising money. Furthermore Mr. Minnich's work is meeting with success. In 1952 the General Brotherhood Board of the denomination reported current receipts from current living donors of $1,071,898.00 in addition to returns from endowment interest, bequests, matured annuities and fulfilled special contracts amounting to $109,095.00. This latter figure constitutes more than one-tenth of the amount given by living donors.

In the 1952-53 issue of *Stewardship Facts* published yearly by the Joint Department of Stewardship and Benevolence, Minnich contributed a significant article on the subject, "A Local Church Considers Wills." He makes several suggestions as to how the pastor can promote the stewardship of accumulated possessions. The foundation is stewardship teaching. A man's last will and testament is more likely to be Christian if he has been a practicing steward during life. Sermons on stewardship with the emphasis on the use of capital wealth will help people to see that stewardship may be fulfilled in life or in death, but must be arranged during life. A union conference on wills would be advisable. Co-operation from denominational representatives can be obtained, for the church boards, colleges and institutions which rightly anticipate capital gifts usually have a representative who will render service when a local church sets up a capital giving emphasis. Use of literature is also helpful. Many pastors maintain a literature rack with material on wills and estate giving. Others see that literature is directed to select people. "In the name of God. Amen!" is an inscription which heads many an ancient will. Quite a few wills now being drawn speak concerning the testator's faith and gratefulness to God. Some contain a clause reading: "Lastly, God has been good to me. In acknowledgment and gratefulness I have remembered the Christian Church and her institutions in my last will and testament."

In emphasizing the stewardship of accumulated possessions Minnich's department has put out four attractive and challenging pamphlets entitled: *Church Annuity Is a Double Blessing, When You Reap the Harvest, Life's Sunset Can Leave an Afterglow,* and *Today's Woman and Her Money.*

The last mentioned pamphlet brings out some startling facts about today's woman as follows: She owns 70 per cent of the wealth of this country, 50 per cent of the stock in industrial corporations, 40 per cent of all the real estate, is the beneficiary of 80 per cent of all life insurance, spends up to 85 per cent of the family income, outlives man by an average of 4½ years. It is the woman in 75 per cent of the cases (based on figures of charitable organizations) who must make final settlement of estates.

The stewardship of accumulated possessions is truly a new emphasis and one that needs to be developed.

IV. THE CHRISTIAN AND MISSIONARY ALLIANCE

The Christian and Missionary Alliance is an evangelistic and missionary movement founded by the Rev. A. B. Simpson, in New York, in 1887. This organization does a great piece of missionary work. It stresses "the deeper Christian life and consecration to the Lord's service." The 1953 edition of the *Yearbook of American Churches* listed the then current numerical strength of this denomination as 510 churches and a membership of 56,077.

In reply to questions submitted in 1943 by the author, the Rev. H. E. Nelson, then Home Secretary of this denomination, replied that "the privilege and responsibilities of stewardship and the joy of sacrificial giving were inherent in the spiritual birth of the movement" thus there has never existed a need to raise the question of stewardship. The entire program of the church has "always been on the free-will offering basis," said Nelson. There is no department of stewardship in the Society. Every local pastor teaches and practices the principles of Christian stewardship and trains the membership of his congregation in the spiritual art of giving, wrote the Home Secretary. Since "tithes and offerings" is a basic principle among their constituents, no legislative plan or program has ever been adopted to promote tithing, for there has never been the need of such a plan, declared the Rev. Nelson.

All official workers and the official organ of the Society, *The Alliance Weekly*, stress tithing. "This scriptural and spiritual ministry of stewardship is a very vital part of the spiritual existence of both our leaders, pastors, and members," asserted Secretary Nelson.

As evidence the letter cited the contributions of some 43,000 members and adherents during 1943 which amounted to $18.07 per capita for foreign missions alone, in addition to the regular giving through church channels for general and special needs. These accomplishments, wrote Nelson, were on a "voluntary basis and in keeping with our teachings on stewardship."

In 1954 the author once again wrote to Mr. Nelson to ascertain the present status of stewardship in the Christian and Missionary Alliance. He reiterated the fact that tithing and Christian Stewardship are principles inherent in the doctrinal position of the Society and in its membership and that "all but an inconsequential few, tithe and give offerings in addition to the regular tithe."

The Alliance pastors regularly give messages on tithing and Christian Stewardship, many being supported on a free-will offering basis and by the tithes of the people. Foreign missions are stressed to the membership which requires offerings for this purpose in excess of the tithe, wrote Nelson.

He pointed out that in addition to all expenses of the churches programs the membership of a little over 60,000 contributed to foreign missions in 1953 more than $2,500,000.00 through the General Fund and approximately $500,000.00 to the designated missionary Specials. On this basis it is calculated that the Alliance membership including the non-wage earners have given $44.50 per capita, said the letter. Nelson thus pointed out that "the issue of tithes, offerings and Christian Stewardship are kept alive week in and week out in the churches of the Christian and Missionary Alliance."

The two splendid letters from Mr. Nelson are very enlightening with regard to what can be done by a group of people who take their stewardship seriously. No other denomination had reached a higher per capita rate of giving for foreign missions when in 1943 the CMA averaged $18.07. The 1953 giving to foreign missions, $44.50 per capita, was an even more remarkable record. In fact it is more than the per capita gifts of most of the major denominations for all purposes. Comparing these records with the per capita gifts recorded for foreign missions by forty-seven denominations reporting last year to *Statistics of Giving,* we find the following comparisons:

Christian and Missionary Alliance per capita $44.50
Seventh day Adventist per capita $31.98
Conference of Evangelical Mennonites per capita $27.64

Another contrast is seen in the fact that whereas the Christian and Missionary Alliance per capita was $44.50 in 1953, the average per capita gifts for foreign missions of forty-seven other denominations was $1.45.

Thus, the Christian and Missionary Alliance which hitherto has not reported to the yearly Statistics of Giving published by the Joint Department of Stewardship and Benevolence really stands at the head of all the denominations in per capita gifts for foreign missions. According to these figures each member of that little denomination last year gave 30.68 times as much for foreign missions as the average church member in forty-seven other denominations.

V. CHURCH OF GOD

The Church of God with headquarters at Anderson, Indiana, is one of the largest of the groups using the name "Church of God." It originated about 1880 and is now emphasizing Christian Unity. As reported in the 1953 edition of the *Yearbook of American Churches* this denomination in 1952 had 1,989 churches and 111,011 members.

In reply to the author's inquiry, the Rev. C. W. Hatch, the Executive Secretary, replied that stewardship was emphasized in his denomination "very, very little until about 1930." R. L. Berry, who was then the secretary of our Church of God World Service, began to publish literature emphasizing stewardship in general and tithing in particular. The agency mentioned above is the department which handles stewardship materials, and encourages stewardship education in the Church of God. Mr.

Hatch presently directs the functions which consist in raising money for the various missionary, educational, and benevolent agencies of the church with stewardship constituting a part of that responsibility.

Mr. Hatch explains the tithing system emphasized in his denomination. The individual is urged to give one-tenth of his income through the local church and in turn the local church is encouraged to give one-tenth of its income to the Church of God World Service.

The Church of God offers to its constituency three attractive stewardship tracts entitled: *The Stewardship Obligation,* by A. F. Gray; *Christian Tithing — A Privilege,* a reprint of one of Robert E. Speer's writings; and *Where Shall the Tithe Go?*

Hatch has recently written a book, *Stewardship Enriches Life,* which has been described as "a refreshing re-emphasis of the biblical doctrine of stewardship applied to every day life."

Hatch recently informed the author of a new development in his church, namely the instituting of a Stewardship Reading Course for ministers in which books, study guides, questions and answers for book appraisal, etc. are provided by the Church of God World Service. Using a rotation system, in a period of twenty-four weeks eight men have read eight books on stewardship and each has submitted an appraisal. Each year between forty-eight and ninety-six readers are sought.

VI. CHURCH OF THE NAZARENE

The Church of the Nazarene is one of the larger holiness bodies. It was organized in Pilot Point, Texas, October, 1908. It is in general accord with the earlier doctrines of Methodism and emphasizes entire sanctification. According to the 1953 Yearbook of American Churches this body in 1953 reported 3,710 churches with 243,152 members.

C. Warren Jones, Stewardship Secretary of the Church of the Nazarene in 1943, submitted a statement regarding his denomination which stated that "stewardship has been emphasized among the Nazarenes ever since we have been a church." The General Stewardship Committee attempts to further the cause of Stewardship in the church through the printed page, including tracts, articles and all periodicals. Mr. Jones stated in his letter that Nazarene people are urged to tithe for it is the Scriptural plan and he feels sure that 70 per cent of the people of his church do tithe.

In recent years the stewardship record of the Church of the Nazarene has attracted the attention of other Christian leaders. In 1952 the Church of the Nazarene reported $117.97 per capita.

Typical of the comments of Christian leaders concerning Nazarene stewardship is a statement found on the inside back cover of the *Fellowship of Tithers* booklet, published by the Church of the Brethren, which states that "evangelism and stewardship are twin forces of great worth" and the Nazarenes have proven it by their increased membership of 38% in the last ten years and per capita giving increase of 179% in the same ten-year period. "A remarkable missionary zeal is evidenced, also, among the Nazarenes," says the article, "by the record of 151 new churches organized in 1952, or one every 58 hours." The statement credits tithing with being "the chief factor in Nazarene strength."

S. T. Ludwig is the present Stewardship Secretary of the Church of the Nazarene with headquarters at 2923 Troost Ave., Kansas City 41, Kansas. He informed the author that a program of stewardship education is carried on constantly among his people, with two annual church-wide offerings for world evangelism at Easter and Thanksgiving, to afford the people an opportunity to make their gifts of love beyond the tithe.

The primary method of the Nazarenes in securing finance for the operation of the denomination locally has traditionally been through tithes and offerings. Tracts, pamphlets and articles are made available to pastors for use in their churches. Pastors are urged to preach frequently on this "vital theme of stewardship as it relates to our program of world evangelism," said Mr. Ludwig.

A bi-monthly publication called, *The Nazarene Pastor,* compiled by the General Stewardship Committee, devotes two or three pages to stewardship.

The "ten per cent program," meaning a tithe of the total giving of a local congregation designated for the general budget of the denomination for world evangelism, has been inaugurated as a minimum goal. Supplemented with the two special offerings, the expansion program of home and foreign missionary endeavor has been underwritten.

At the General Assembly in 1948 a "Crusade for Souls" was inaugurated with the principal purpose being "to stimulate and encourage the investment of time and talents as related to stewardship."

More of the Nazarene secrets of success in the promotion of stewardship will be found in an article by Ludwig entitled: "Stewardship Facts, 1954-55," in his comments on the subject, *The Stewardship Tradition of the Church of the Nazarene.* "The only adequate motivating impulse for all of our labor is love toward God in response to his matchless love," states Ludwig. This responding love is evidenced in outpoured, selfless service. Ludwig states the Nazarene's belief in giving one-tenth of their income to the Kingdom of God through the church as God's minimum standard for the Christian. Offerings above tithes are encouraged as investments in building the kingdom.

The Nazarene organization has a General Stewardship Committee which, Mr. Ludwig explains, is composed of general officers, the six department secretaries, the editor of the denominational paper and the editor-in-chief of Sunday School literature. The task of this Committee is to integrate the emphasis placed upon stewardship among all groups and all levels of instruction coming from the general headquarters.

On the district level is a Committee on Stewardship which endeavors to interpret and apply the stewardship principles in the church's program. In the local church a Board of Stewards is assigned specific duties, including the cultivation of the stewardship program within the local church, involving wealth, time and talents.

The techniques employed may be summarized thus. In Stewardship Education, literature for study and distribution is made available. February of each year is designated as stewardship month with emphasis via the major periodicals, preaching and teaching. *The Nazarene Pastor* is published bi-monthly for ministers. Pastors are urged to give frequent messages to the people involving the stewardship privilege and obligation. The Christian Service Training program is for the purpose of promoting training courses in the field of Christian stewardship. In the matter of raising money, all the churches are urged to tithe as a minimum for world evangelism, which becomes the regular "breadline budget" for the Nazarene's world mission program.

In addition to the regular month by month program emphasized above, there are the two inspirational church-wide offerings each year, at Easter and during the Thanksgiving season, in which people are urged to give with a "plus" as the Lord has prospered them to further missions at home and abroad. In 1952 these offerings totalled $605,261.44 for Easter and $625,550.71 for Thanksgiving.

In the general budget of the denomination, there has been set aside about a quarter million dollars for direct aid in home mission churches. Therefore the largest amount of giving to this fund comes from the several districts themselves. Here the stronger churches give aid to the weaker ones and for the establishment of new churches. The fact that this money is raised in the local units within the district and expended on that district under the supervision of a home mission board, has stimu-

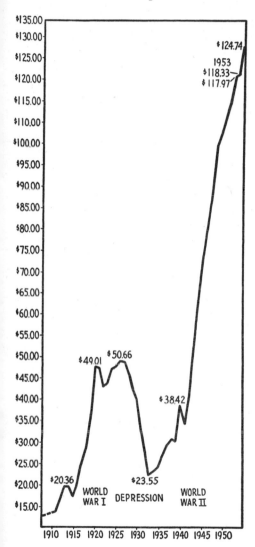

FIGURE 11. PER CAPITA GIVING IN THE CHURCH OF THE NAZARENE (1908-1954) based on: (1) the annual reports of the Church of the Nazarene and of the United Stewardship Council as cited in 1954-55 **Stewardship Facts** (1908-1950), and (2) the annual reports of the Joint Department of Stewardship and Benevolence (1951-1954).

lated the Nazarene people to give gladly for these purposes because they see the results near at hand.

A Prayer and Fasting League exists within the church. The men and women who join this league agree to fast, if possible, one meal each week and give the price of that meal for world evangelism. Last year there were 72,357 members and the amount of money received from this source was $280,813.28.

The Church of the Nazarene furnishes to its constituency twelve attractive pamphlets on the various phases of stewardship and tithing. The accompanying graph which has been worked out from the yearly denominational statistics of the Church of the Nazarene gives a bird's-eye view of stewardship results in this denomination since its founding in 1908 through 1954. Notice how the giving of Nazarenes has climbed in the last few years to the remarkable figure of $124.74 per capita for all purposes in 1954.

VII. THE EVANGELICAL MISSION COVENANT CHURCH OF AMERICA

The Evangelical Mission Covenant Church of America is "a transplantation of a free church missionary movement in the Swedish state church to the United States in 1885." Until recently the name has been Swedish Evangelical Mission Covenant Church.

The 1953 *Yearbook of American Churches* shows that in 1953 this denomination reported 489 churches, and a membership of 51,850.

Edgar E. Swanson was the Secretary of Stewardship in 1943 and informed the author that the Mission Covenant Church has throughout its entire history given a strong emphasis to Christian stewardship. The first official action was taken in June of 1942 when an office was designated for that purpose. Tithing or "proportionate giving is emphasized in all stewardship writings." Swanson estimates that "about one-tenth of our people return to the Lord at least one-tenth of their income."

To promote stewardship youth leaders join in the emphasis in their educational material; Vacation Bible School carries a strong stewardship emphasis. In June 1942 the Covenant Tither's movement was launched to appeal to youth. The Sunday just prior to Thanksgiving Day has been designated as national stewardship Sunday and a pamphlet entitled *Accepting Partnership With God* was published.

The literature is very attractive and readable and is of high quality both as to the content of the messages contained and as to printing.

The Stewardship Secretary of the Evangelical Mission Covenant Church is to be commended on having launched the Covenant Tither's movement among the young people of the denomination, who will be the future leaders of the church. This is a pioneer movement which other denominations would do well to pattern.

The designation of the Sunday before Thanksgiving as National Stewardship Sunday is another move worthy of comment. Suppose all the denominations would follow this example, designating the Sunday before Thanksgiving as Stewardship Sunday, and distribute Stewardship literature on that Sunday. What an impact such action would make for stewardship emphasis!

The man in charge of the promotion of stewardship in the Evangelical Mission Covenant Church of America in 1955 was the Rev. Joseph C. Danielson, 5101 North Francisco Ave., Chicago 25, Ill.

VIII. EVANGELICAL AND REFORMED CHURCH

The Evangelical and Reformed Church was formed on June 26, 1934, by a union of the Evangelical Synod of North America and the Reformed Church in the United States, at Cleveland, Ohio. The union was unique in that it left the details to be adjusted after the transaction. The constitution was declared in effect at the General Synod which met at Lancaster, Pennsylvania, in June, 1940. The boards merged and reorganized and on February 1, 1941, took over the work carried on by the two former denominations.

The 1941 *Yearbook of American Churches* shows that in 1939 this body had 2,861 churches. In its report to the Joint Department of Stewardship and Benevolence for the year ending December 31, 1952 this body showed 752,144 members.

Thomas Kane, otherwise known as Layman, in the last book which he wrote before his death, *Adventures in Tithing*, tells of having received a letter from William E. Lampe, then Secretary of the Department of Stewardship of the Reformed Church, dated December 23, 1919. It referred to a meeting of the United Missionary and Stewardship Committee of the General Synod where Kane's extensive free literature ministry was discussed and a vote of thanks extended for the "great help" he had rendered through the gifts of literature on tithing. The Committee agreed that "Layman" Kane had probably done more to advance the cause of stewardship and to emphasize the law of the tithe than any other man in America.

The man in charge of the promotion of stewardship in the Evangelical and Reformed Church in 1955 was James W. Bright, D.D., Executive Secretary of the Commission of Stewardship, 2969 West 25th St., Cleveland 13, Ohio.

In response to the author's inquiries concerning the present status of stewardship in his denomination, Bright replied that in 1945-46 his denomination conducted an aggressive Stewardship Enlistment of time, talent, and treasure which was the "upturn of real benevolence growth."

New methods of stewardship promotion include visual aids, graphs, field representatives, more effective literature, stewardship institutes and lay workers' conference. Mr. Bright spoke of the new emphasis on stewardship of time and talent and on wills and annuities; Sector Plan developed by American Baptists; Wells Organization in church fund raising; and "Christian tithing motivated by love rather than legalism." The Commission of Stewardship at the present time has no less than 103 pieces of literature on stewardship and tithing.

IX. The Evangelical and United Brethren Church

This body had its origin in Johnstown, Pennsylvania, November 16, 1946, in the consummation of the organic union between the Evangelical Church and the United Brethren in Christ. Both these former communions had their beginnings in Pennsylvania in the evangelistic movement of the early nineteenth century. Jacob Albright was the founder of the Evangelical Church and Dr. Philip William Otterbein founded the United Brethren Church in 1800. The doctrine is Armenian and the government Methodistic. The denomination has 4,291 churches and 654,594 members.

A. Stewardship in the Evangelical Branch

In 1943 Dr. A. F. Weaver was the Stewardship Secretary of the Evangelical Church as well as Executive Secretary-Treasurer of the denomination. He advises that previous to the General Conference which met in Naperville, Illinois, October, 1942, stewardship was promoted under the auspices of the Missionary Society of the Evangelical Church with the field secretary of the Missionary Society having direct charge of the work. However, the General Conference decided to place the work under the direction of the executive secretary-treasurer of the General Administrative Council because it was felt that stewardship should be promoted by the agency related to all other boards and agencies of the denomination.

Tithing is emphasized by the United Brethren church, asserts Dr. Weaver, it being a definite part of the program of denominational stewardship promotion. Particular mention is made of the Women's Missionary Society and its auxiliaries as sources of tithe emphasis.

B. Stewardship in The Church of the United Brethren Branch

In 1943 in reply to the author's inquiry D. T. Gregory, the

Executive Secretary of this denomination, took the time to compose a splendid report concerning the status of stewardship in his denomination at the time. He indicated that the major stewardship emphasis of his denomination followed the General Conference in 1913 when a Finance Commission with a Secretary of Stewardship was elected.

Presently the Stewardship Department is under the Board of Administration. The period between Easter and Pentecost is designated for stewardship study. Pastors are asked to plan along such lines as: (1) classes for studying the practical phases of Christian stewardship, with the textbook being *Will A Man Rob God?*, by Bishop Cushman, (2) a series of sermons on stewardship requirements and blessings, (3) study of stewardship principles in Sunday School substituting it for three or four regular lessons, (4) a short stewardship play presented by the young people, (5) distribution of helpful stewardship literature, (6) stewardship slides during a few evening services, and (7) an enlistment service at the close of the study period.

Tithing is emphasized in the E.U.B. denomination and Mr. Gregory reports that during the last calendar year a 21 per cent increase in enrolled tithers was realized.

Stewardship materials are incorporated in a series of brief messages which are printed in teacher's quarterlies for adult and young people's work as a special "Stewardship Application of the Lesson."

One phase of the work of the United Brethren in Christ during this period which deserves special comment, is its study course of four lessons entitled, *Following Christ, the Key to Steward ship*. The course is made up similar to a Sunday School lesson quarterly. Scripture passages dealing with stewardship form the basis of the lesson. A golden text is given. The central truth is pointed out. Bible readings for the week are also given. The exposition of the lesson follows.

C. *Stewardship in the Evangelical United Brethren Church Since the Union in 1946*

The man who is in charge of the promotion of stewardship in The Evangelical and United Brethren Church in 1955 was the Executive Secretary, L. L. Baugman, D.D. with headquarters at 1444 Knott Bldg., Dayton 2, Ohio. Mr. Baugman states that his denomination does not conduct stewardship campaigns as such, but has "a year-round emphasis and a total program." Their stewardship philosophy "includes all of life," he remarked, and stewardship principles are employed to unify and correlate the total program of the church. New methods employed during the last several years include 16 mm sound movies, sound film strips, turn-over charts, stewardship packets, stewardship standard and work shops.

The average per capita giving for missions and for benevolence before the union of the two denominations was $5.00 while the average now is $8.00. An even greater increase is seen in giving for all purposes which before the union was $24.00 per capita, but now is $45.00 per capita.

X. AMERICAN LUTHERAN CHURCH

The American Lutheran Church is a constituent body of the American Lutheran Conference. It was created as the result of a merger of three Lutheran groups in 1930; namely the Evangelical Lutheran Joint Synod of Ohio and Other States (organized 1918), The Evangelical Lutheran Synod of Iowa and Other States (organized 1854), and The Lutheran Synod of Buffalo (organized 1845).

This denomination has about 2000 churches and according to the report submitted to the Joint Department of Stewardship and Benevolence for the year ending December 31, 1952 there were 541,250 members (excluding infants).

The Rev. Wm. G. Sodt, D.D., as the Stewardship Secretary of this denomination in 1943, informed the author that his church "immediately developed a program with emphasis on Stewardship," after its organization. The Department of Stewardship and Finance was organized in 1930 but "is not a money raising department in the strictest sense of the word," says Dr. Sodt. A program of stewardship "to set a spiritual background for Christian giving," is being developed. Secretary Sodt commented: "We do not emphasize tithing as tithing but we advocate a program called the separated portion."

One of the officials of the Department of Stewardship and Finance of the American Lutheran Church is George S. Schultz. In *Stewardship Facts 1954-55* Schultz writes under the caption: "Ambassadors for Christ" and declares that stewardship is "not a spasmodic act of periodic giving" but rather is a "way of life."

XI. MENNONITE CHURCH

The Mennonite Church represents the largest group of Mennonites who began arriving in the United States as early as 1683, settling in Germantown, Pennsylvania. They derive their name from Menno Simons, their outstanding leader born in 1496. The 1953 *Yearbook of American Churches* shows that this body then had 477 churches and 61,811 members.

A. J. Metzler, the General Manager of the Mennonite Publishing House, who was first contacted in 1943 replied that stewardship is "not officially emphasized" in his denomination but is attributed to individual speakers and writers. Thus no organization or office on stewardship is maintained. Many of the Mennonite ministers teach tithing and it is practiced by some of the members though not officially endorsed, explained Mr. Metzler.

In reply to the author's recent inquiry as to the present status of stewardship in the Mennonite Church, Metzler wrote that the most significant thing his denomination has done in the way of stewardship in recent years was the establishment of the Conrad Grebel Lectures by the Board of Education, under the leadership of president Nelson E. Kauffman of Hannibal, Mo. Each year $2,000 or more is made available for an outstanding Mennonite scholar to devote approximately six months in research and study in the preparation of a series of lectures on some significant question. The subject of Stewardship was assigned to Milo Kauffman of the Hesston College in Hesston, Kansas. "Brother Kauffman has done an outstanding piece of work and is delivering his lectures throughout our church," commented Mr. Metzler.

This is a significant development in the area of stewardship education, being the first case that has come to the attention of the author concerning a denomination offering a scholarship for research and completion of his findings in a series of lectures.

Copies of Milo Kauffman's lectures appeared monthly in the new Mennonite magazine, *Christian Living*, under such titles as: "Partnership with God," "God Is Still the Owner," "How Much Does the Steward Owe," "Is Tithing Practical Today?," and "The Stewardship of Life."

Introducing his series of studies on Stewardship, in the chapter entitled "Partner with God," Mr. Kauffman declares that "A revival of Christian stewardship will inevitably mean a revival of spiritual life, and a revival of spiritual life always means a revival of Christian stewardship," in the life of the individual, the local church, or of the church at large. He adds that "Christian stewardship, right relationship with God, holiness of life, fellowship with God, victorious living, and the consecrated life are as dependent upon each other as are the spokes in a wheel."

Mr. Kauffman defines stewardship as "the practice of systematic proportionate giving of time, abilities, and material possessions, based on a conviction that these are a trust from God to be used in His service, for the benefit of all mankind."

Kauffman observes: "We become Christ's stewards when He becomes our Lord. To acknowledge the Lordship of Christ means that we accept stewardship."

XII. UNITED PRESBYTERIAN CHURCH

The United Presbyterian Church dates back to the Reformed Presbyterian (Covenanter) Church in 1643 and the Associate Presbyterian (Seceder) Church in 1733, both of Scotland. These two groups appeared in America in 1774 and 1753 respectively. They united and became the Associate Reformed Presbyterian Church in 1782. A minority, however, continued as the Associate Presbyterian Church but in 1858 the two groups united and became the United Presbyterian Church.

The 1953 *Yearbook of American Churches* shows that this denomination had 829 churches and an inclusive membership of 222,201 of which 180,622 are thirteen years and older.

Thomas Kane, previously mentioned as one of the pioneers of the tithing movement, came from The Associate Reformed Church, which was one of the bodies that united to form the United Presbyterian Church. Kane testified that his parents were members of the Associate Reformed Church and that as a child "David's Psalms, Rouse's version, and the shorter catechism were as familiar to me as the multiplication table."

Because of Mr. Kane's early connection with this denomination it was one of the first to receive free tithing literature from him. In his *Adventures in Tithing,* Kane mentions having sent out some of the initial tithing literature to the United Presbyterian Church during the nineties.

A business man in Pittsburgh, in behalf of a special committee selected by the General Assembly of the United Presbyterian Church, arranged with Layman Kane to wrap and mail packages of tithing pamphlets entitled *What We Owe and How to Pay It* for distribution of a copy to every family in the denomination throughout the United States. A list of names and addresses of all the ministers and the number of pamphlets to be wrapped was provided. "While the membership of the United Presbyterian Church has always been noted for liberality, especially in missions," noted the Layman, "statistics show that this thorough circulation of this tithing literature produced a large and permanent increase in that Church for the Master's work."

In 1920 Dr. J. E. White, the Stewardship Secretary of the United Presbyterian Church ordered 100,000 Layman tithing pamphlets to be distributed in his denomination. In the same years ministers of the United Presbyterian Church ordered about 50,000 pamphlets direct.

The *Epworth Herald,* for July 17, 1920, carried an item stating that the United Presbyterian Church has established new standards of giving by subscribing an average of more than $21 per member annually for missions and educational purposes for the ensuing five years. "This year has witnessed by far the greatest financial advance in missionary giving ever made by Protestant Churches," asserted the article.

On November 1, 1920 Dr. White wrote Layman (Thomas Kane) accepting his offer of literature at one-half the cost of printing, and placed an order for ten thousand each of the following pamphlets: *Mine and Thine, Talks with Money, Thanksgiving Ann, Is the Tithe a Debt?, Aunt Margaret's Tenth, A Tithing Catechism, Does Tithing Pay? Who Owns the World?* and *The Deacon's Tenth;* in addition to one thousand copies of *Adventures in Tithing.* Dr. White commented that the United Presbyterians were pushing the stewardship campaign to be "stronger than ever" that year. Literature was being "fed" to the congregations and stewardship study classes suggested the enrollment of tithing stewards to be continued.

The above historical material is interesting because of the light they throw on Thomas Kane's (Layman) contribution to the stewardship movement within the United Presbyterian Church. We now turn our attention to a statement of the Executive Secretary of the Board of Adminstration of the United Presbyterian Church, T. C. Strangeway, who in 1943 wrote that "stewardship has always been emphasized in our denomination from the time missionaries came to our country from Scotland as representatives of the Associate and the Reformed Churches."

The agency having charge of stewardship organization and promotion is the Board of Administration which under different titles has been in existence for over fifty years. Strangeway attributes the leadership of his church in the field of stewardship to its "emphasis upon tithing and missions."

The Every Member Canvass and offering envelopes were promoted by the United Presbyterian Church before they were common in most churches, claims Mr. Strangeway.

It has been the privilege of the author to have an interview with Dr. John E. Simpson, pastor of the First United Presbyterian Church of Oak Park, Ill. Dr. Simpson has written the following books on stewardship: *This Grace Also, He That Giveth, This World's Goods, Into My Storehouse* (A Cyclopedia), *Faithful Also in Much,* and *A Lad's Lunch.*

In the last title Dr. Simpson collaborated with W. J. H. McKnight, D.D., pastor on leave from the United Presbyterian

Church of Kenmore, New York, and Chaplain in the United States Army. *A Lad's Lunch,* published by the Layman Foundation, consists of a series of stewardship stories intended for use in teaching children between the ages of 8 and 15. Dr. McKnight wrote the graded memory work to be used with these stories. This little volume of 48 pages is a new venture in the field of stewardship to reach the young. Dr. Simpson's most popular book is *This Grace Also.*

The United Presbyterian Church has pioneered in promoting Stewardship Essay Contests among the young people of its denomination. In 1942 over 2600 young people throughout the denomination took part in the contest.

The Stewardship Contest for 1943 was arranged for three age groups and cash awards were given to the winner. *Group A* (18-22 years) was required to prepare manuscripts of at least 1000 words on the topic, *Tithing Stewards and Financing God's Work. Group B* took in young people between the ages of 15 and 17 with a minimum of 900 words on the assigned topic, *Winning Others to Christ and Honest Stewardship of Possession. Group C* took in young people between the ages of 12 to 14 and they were required to write manuscripts of at least 700 words on the topic, *My Money and My Life.*

Each contestant received a large envelope containing the rules of the contest for his particular group and a slip with the assigned topic and Scriptures for special study in preparation in writing the essay. It also contained four choice tracts, a form on which to sign a tithing covenant, and an enrollment card. The tracts included in the Stewardship Packet for *Group A* were: Helen Kingsbury Wallace, *Money-Raising or Stewardship, The Sin We Are Afraid to Mention* (a reprint from the *Sunday School Times*), *Stewardship of Tithing,* and *Figuring the Tithe.*

The *Essay Contest* method of promoting stewardship has much merit in that the approach is indirect and young people are influenced during the ages when life decisions are usually made.

Emphasis on tithing early in the history of the denomination and persistent and intelligent promotion of stewardship and missions explains the splendid record the United Presbyterians have made in giving to benevolences.

Chapter XVI
THE STEWARDSHIP STORY SUMMARIZED AND CONCLUDED

I. Summary

THE TERM stewardship does not seem to have occurred in colonial literature or records of that day. Coming from countries of the old world, it was a new concept for most of the colonists to build their own churches and support their ministers. Since there was no widespread missionary activity the records of church finances in those days were concerned mainly with the problem of ministerial support.

The early part of the nineteenth century is significant in stewardship history because of the rise of Modern Missions. The close relation between missions and stewardship is seen in that the emphasis on missions eventually brought about a stewardship awakening. Missions called attention to needs. Stewardship received increasing emphasis as godly men thought through the problem of meeting the needs of the missionary challenge.

The Civil War had a disastrous effect upon the stewardship emphasis. The great stewardship literature of the eighteen fifties was allowed to lapse. In many quarters covetousness reigned during the reconstruction period.

Then a new thing happened. The Student Volunteer Movement came into existence. Again missions received their rightful attention and the stewardship emphasis once more prospered.

The period marking the close of the nineteenth century and the opening of the twentieth is notable in the history of stewardship because of the emphasis tithing received. It was in the nineties that Thomas Kane, otherwise know as Layman, began to circulate tithing literature in large quantities. The Storehouse Tithing plan was born, and many tithing organizations sprung up in America. In England, Henry Lansdell published his monumental work, *The Sacred Tenth,* which was read on both sides of the Atlantic.

In 1906 The Layman's Missionary Movement came into being which, as the name implies, promoted missions among laymen. The Layman's Movement emphasized stewardship in general and tithing in particular and advocated the introduction of the every-member-canvass and the use of duplex envelopes.

147

In 1914, Harvey Reeves wrote his stewardship classis, *A Man and His Money.*

In 1915 Ralph S. Cushman (later bishop of the Saint Paul Area of the Methodist Church) emerged in the stewardship movement. He made history when he led the members of the Geneva Methodist Church of Geneva, New York, to adopt tithing. He was chosen Executive Secretary of the Department of Stewardship in the Joint Centenary Celebration of the Methodists. Then he became the Executive Secretary of the Department of Stewardship in the Interchurch World Movement, and finally was elected president of the newly organized United Stewardship Council of the Churches of Christ in America.

The period which followed the close of World War I will be remembered in the stewardship story as the era of great financial drives. The Disciples had led the way with the Men and Millions Movement during World War I. Then in rapid succession the year 1919 saw the launching of the New Era Movement by the Presbyterians, the New World Movement by the American Baptists (then known as Northern Baptists), the 75 Million Campaign of the Southern Baptists and the Centenary Celebration of the Methodists, with a goal of "A Million Tithers in Methodism."

Then came the era of controversy. The collapse of the Interchurch World Movement left the Mission boards of the larger denominations in debt. The Fundamentalist-Modernist controversy raged in more than one denomination creating a spirit of bitterness and suspicion that proved to be a poor environment for stewardship and generosity.

After controversy came depression. The crash of the stock market brought the curtailment of stewardship activities. Giving for missions and for all purposes showed a sharp decline in all denominations. But even the cloud of depression had its bright lining. Out of the depression experiences came three stewardship plans: The Lord's Acre Plan for people in rural areas; The Lord's Hour Plan, an adaption of The Lord's Acre Plan to the conditions of the city church; and the Belmont (Tithe) Plan operating in hundreds of rural and city churches.

The period of World War II proved to be another era of decline in stewardship emphasis. Again there was a lapse in the printing of stewardship literature. The old literature was depleted and materials were not produced to take its place. The energies of the nation's leaders were concentrated on the one objective of winning the war.

The immediate post war period proved to be another season of campaign which was generally called crusades. The Southern

Baptists led out with the Centennial Crusade. American Baptists put on the World Mission Crusade. The Disciples promulgated The Crusade for a Christian World of Disciples, while the Methodists sponsored The Crusade for Christ and The Presbyterian Church in the United States (Southern) promoted the Program of Progress.

It is good to know that The Layman Tithing Foundation inaugurated by the late Thomas Kane is still functioning in the good purpose which it was founded, that is the distribution of great quantities of literature on tithing. However, the work of this foundation needs to be strengthened with greater financial resources and its literature needs to be continually renewed and brought up to date from the standpoint of the printer's art.

It is also of interest to know that the United States Stewardship Council, which for more than thirty years carried forward its work of stewardship education and the compiling of stewardship statistics, was in 1951 merged into what is now known as the Joint Department of Stewardship and Benevolence. This newly formed organization, under the energetic leadership of its Executive Secretary, the Rev. T. K. Thompson, is now carrying on in an expanded ministry the work begun by the United Stewardship Council.

It is interesting to see the vitality of the Storehouse Tithing Plan. This plan first made tithing meaningful in Wesley Chapel and in the Geneva Methodist Church in New York state. Though not promoted as such by any particular organization or secretary the popularity of this plan is seen in that it is still used in many churches, though in an adapted way. One of the churches that is using an adapted form of the Storehouse Tithing Plan is the Highland Park Baptist Church in Chattanooga, Tennessee. With some 2000 enrolled tithers the church no doubt has the distinction of having the largest number of tithers on record in one church at the present time.

It is also encouraging to know that The Lord's Acre Plan which has had such a noble history is still continuing to meet stewardship needs in hundreds of rural churches throughout the length and breadth of our land and is being expanded to meet the needs of mission fields. It is good to know that the kindred Belmont Plan continues to be used.

Of the major denominations the largest per capita gifts for all purposes were recorded by The Presbyterian Church in the United States (Southern) when in 1954 this denomination reached an all time high of $75.54 per capita for all purposes. The Lutheran Church — Missouri Synod was a close second when in 1954 it recorded for all purposes $67.82 per capita. In benevolence giving Southern Presbyterians among the larger denominations have taken a leading place, though the highest gifts for benevolence was reached by the Lutheran Church — Missouri Synod in 1952 with $19.40 per capita.

Among the stewardship personalities of the larger denominations Dr. Earle V. Pierce of the American Baptists stands out. His lectures on stewardship to the students of the Baptist seminaries of both the North and the South have done much to make the present generation of Baptist ministers stewardship conscious, and his splendid book *The Supreme Beatitude* has had a tremendous circulation.

Of the larger denominations, the Southern Baptist Convention, has without a doubt made the greatest progress in stewardship education. The 1953 record of 10,000 churches with 700,000 people spending a whole week in the study of stewardship is notable. In the same year the total number of tithers enlisted was raised to 804,374. It is doubtful if one denomination has ever enlisted a larger number of tithers. Never before has stewardship been promoted on such a large scale and never has a large denomination made so much progress along stewardship lines as Southern Baptists during the past fifteen years.

In 1936 Southern Baptists occupied the lowest place among five major denominations in contributions to missionary and benevolent causes having given in that year a total of $4,624,515. In 1953 Southern Baptists occupied the first place among all the major denominations in contributions to missionary and benevolent causes having given in that year $48,427,760.

The stewardship story in the smaller denominations has also demanded attention.

The Baptist General Conference in 1952 made the splendid record of giving $23.00 per capita to missions. In addition this body has made a contribution to stewardship education by the production of a new book on stewardship, entitled *The Divine Economy,* written by Dr. Alphin Conrad, professor in Bethel Seminary, St. Paul, Minnesota, and published in 1954 for use as a text in stewardship in colleges and seminaries.

The Church of the Brethren is doing a significant piece of work, pioneering in the area of the "Stewardship of accumulated possessions." In addition to the usual promotion of stewardship, this denomination through its financial representative, H. Spencer Minnich, has been quite successful in securing bequests and annuities for church institutions and organizations.

The Christian and Missionary Alliance, true to its strong missionary tradition, leads all the denominations in per capita giving to missions, having in 1953 averaged $44.50 per person for that purpose.

The fact that the Church of the Nazarene in 1953 gave $118.33 per capita for all purposes indicates that its leaders are doing a splendid piece of stewardship promotion.

In the Church of the Nazarene not only the tithe is stressed, but offerings as well. In addition to the regular tithe given Sunday by Sunday two great inspirational church-wide offerings for missions are received each year, the one during the Easter season and the other during the Thanksgiving season. It is worthy of note that in 1952 by means of these two offerings the Church of the Nazarene received the magnificant sum of $1,230,-812.15.

Also worthy of note is the Prayer and Fasting league of the Church of the Nazarene, which in 1952 was composed of 72,357 members, each of whom covenanted to give up one meal per week and give the price of it for the work of evangelism. Through this unique medium was raised $280,812 over and above the other giving of the members of this church.

The Mennonite Church is coming to the front in the stewardship story. The move to give a $2,000 scholarship for the Conrad Grebel Lectures to Milo Kauffman, for the purpose of making a thorough study of stewardship and recording his findings for extensive lecturing throughout the denomination is a new approach in stewardship education. We believe this to be a forerunner of good stewardship news from this smaller denomination in years to come.

For total benevolence for 1953 the Methodist Church gave $46,882,218 and the Southern Baptist Convention, which in that year led all the denominations in giving to total benevolences, recorded $48,427,760.

II. Conclusions

Stewardship has been an American contribution to theological thinking. With the eventual separation of church and state came the need for supporting the church and its ever expanding mission with free will offerings. This support at first was weak but through the years has been greatly strengthened by the stewardship concept.

What began as a tiny trickle of truth has grown into a mighty Niagara of power in the conscience and thinking of American Christians. The Biblical principles of stewardship which in the early history of our country were for the most part unknown are now broadcast far and wide by every possible means.

Stewardship emphasis has been a growing matter. The word stewardship does not even appear in the literature of colonial days, while the word tithe had a very definite odium about it to the American colonists because of the historical connections of the word with the corrupt tax systems of the old world church state economy.

The first emphasis in the direction of stewardship had to do with the problem of ministerial support which led to somewhat of a system of giving and to an emphasis on proportionate giving. The idea of proportion in turn brought up the question as to how large the proportion should be. This led to the rediscovery of the Biblical principle of the tithe as the acknowledgment of God's ownership and the minimum standard for Christian giving.

Missions and stewardship have always gone hand in hand. Historically the emphasis on missions preceded the stewardship emphasis. Missions presented the need. Stewardship met the challenge. Through the years the prosperity of the one has been dependent on the other.

Wars have always had an adverse effect on the stewardship emphasis. This was true in connection with the Civil War and also World War I and World War II.

Controversy also has had a disastrous effect on the stewardship emphasis whenever it has raised its ugly head. Controversy creates distrust and dries up the wells of sacrificial giving. In times of controversy giving to benevolences have usually tended to decline.

Stewardship must be taught. The Christian groups that have been the most effective in the promotion of stewardship have magnified the teaching ministry. For the best results stewardship must be taught "line upon line, precept upon precept" in the Sunday School, in the young peoples services, in the worship services, by tracts, by study courses, by books, by audio-visual aids and every possible means.

To make stewardship meaningful the tithe must be stressed. The denominations and Christian groups in which the leaders have taken a strong stand on tithing have made the best records in per capita giving.

Great things have happened in the field of stewardship but greater things are yet to be accomplished. Church leaders who began emphasizing the tithe years ago are just now beginning to see the full fruits of their labors in the larger per capita giving of their respective constituencies.

There is need for a new emphasis in stewardship. Too often stewardship has been used as merely a means of raising money. We need to think of it as a way of bringing Christians into a place of larger usefulness. Stewardship as a means of raising money may become as sounding brass and as a tinkling cymbal. Stewardship as the way to the abundant life rings forth the glorious melody of the Christian and is in full harmony with the Creator.

More emphasis should be given to stewardship in the light of the Lordship of Christ and in the light of His sure return. The faithful steward who lives each day in the light of the coming day of reckoning will be the steward who will hear the welcome words of his Lord, "Well done, thou good and faithful servant."

BIBLIOGRAPHY

A. ORIGINAL SOURCES

I. *Books Published before World War II*

Agar, F. A., *Modern Money Methods*. The Judson Press, Philadelphia, 1921.

———, *Church Profit-Making*. Fleming H. Revell Company, New York, 1929.

Babbs, Arthur V., *The Law of the Tithe*. Fleming H. Revell Company, New York, 1912.

Bacon, *The Christian Doctrine of Stewardship in Respect to Property*. Nathan Whiting, New Haven, 1832.

Barrister, A., *The Universal Obligation of Tithes*. Elliot Stock, London, 1911.

Blair, Herbert E., *Paul, A Christian Financier*. Christian Literature Society of Korea, Korea, 1937.

Block, Karl M., *Our Common Life*. The National Council of the Protestant Episcopal Church Field Department, New York, n.d.

Butler, Clementina, *Ownership*. Fleming H. Revell Company, New York, 1927.

Burroughs, P. E., *Our Church and Ours*. Sunday School Board of the Southern Baptist Convention, Nashville, 1928.

———, *Our Lord and Ours*. Sunday School Board of the Southern Baptist Convention, Nashville, 1928.

———, *The Grace of Giving*. Sunday School Board of the Southern Baptist Convention, Nashville, 1934.

Buttrick, George A., *The Parables of Jesus*. Harper and Brothers, New York, 1928.

Calkins, Harvey Reeves, *Stewardship Starting Points*. The Methodist Book Concern, New York, 1916.

Brown, George W., *Gems of Thought on Tithing*. Jennings and Graham, New York, 1911.

Brown, Ina Corine, *Jesus' Teaching on the Use of Money*. Cokesbury Press, Nashville, 1924.

Cole, Stewart G., *The History of Fundamentalism*. Richard R. Smith, Inc., New York, 1931.

Cook, Charles A., *Stewardship and Missions*. American Baptist Publication Society, Philadelphia, 1908.

Crawford, Julius Earl, *The Call to Christian Stewardship*. Publishing House of the Methodist Episcopal Church, South, Nashville, 1924.

——— , *The Stewardship Life*. Cokesbury Press, Nashville, 1929.

Cushman, Ralph S., *Dealing Squarely With God*. The Abingdon Press, Cincinnati, 1927.

155

————, *Modern Stewardship Sermons.* The Abingdon Press, Cincinnati, 1919.

————, *The Message of Stewardship.* The Abingdon Press, Cincinnati, 1922.

————, *The New Christian Studies in Stewardship,* revised. Interchurch World Movement, New York, 1919.

————, *Will A Man Rob God?* Abingdon-Cokesbury Press, New York, 1942.

Dodd, Monroe E., *Concerning the Collection.* Fleming H. Revell Company, New York, n.d.

Dillard, J. E., *Bible Stewardship.* Executive Committee, Southern Baptist Convention, Nashville, n.d.

Duncan, John Wesley, *Our Christian Stewardship.* Jennings and Graham, Cincinnati, 1909.

Emery, Julia C., *A Century of Endeavor.* Department of Missions of the Protestant Episcopal Church, New York, n.d.

Fahs, Charles H., *Trends in Protestant Giving.* Institute of Social and Religious Research, New York, 1929.

Finney, Charles G., *Lectures on Revivals of Religion,* A New Edition. Fleming H. Revell Company, New York, 1885.

————, *Lectures to Professing Christians.* John W. Taylor, New York, 1837.

Freeman, John D., *More Than Money.* The Sunday School Board of the Southern Baptist Convention, Nashville, 1935.

Henderson, J. T., *Financing A Church.* Sunday School Board of the Southern Baptist Convention, Nashville, 1927.

Hensey, James A., *Storehouse Tithing or Stewardship Up-To-Date.* The Revell Press, New York, 1922.

————, *How Much Shall I Give?* Presbyterian Board of Publication, Philadelphia, n.d.

Huebschmann, J. S., *Three Greater Successes.* Central Publishing House, Cleveland, 1924.

James, Powhatan W., *George W. Truett.* The Macmillan Company, New York, 1939.

————, *Inventory of the Church Archives in New York City, Presbyterian Church in the United States of America.* Historical Records Survey, W.P.A., New York, 1940.

Lovejoy, Luther E., *Speculating in Futures.* The Methodist Book Concern, New York, 1927.

————, *Stewardship for All of Life.* The Methodist Book Concern, New York, 1924.

Leavell, Frank H., *Training in Stewardship.* Sunday School Board of the Southern Baptist Convention, Nashville, 1920.

Long, Roswell C., *Stewardship Parables of Jesus.* Cokesbury Press, Nashville, 1931.

Lowry, Oscar, *Should Christians Tithe?* Glad Tidings Publishing Co., Fort Wayne, n.d.

Luccock, George N., *The Meaning of Stewardship*. The Board of Education of the Presbyterian Church, Philadelphia, 1923.

Lundy, George E., *A Survey of the Layman Foundation*. In manuscript form, not published, 1940.

Lutheran World Almanac. National Lutheran Council, Vols. I to VII, 1921-1933, New York.

McConoughy, David, *Money the Acid Test*. Missionary Education Movement, New York, 1918.

———, *Christian Stewardship*. The Presbyterian Board of Publication, Philadelphia, 1919.

McConnell, Francis John, *Christian Materialism*. Friendship Press, New York, 1936.

Landis, Benson Y., *Yearbook of American Churches*. Federal Council of Churches of Christ, Detroit, 1941.

Melvin, M. E., *Royal Partnership*. Fleming H. Revell Co., New York, 1926.

Morrill, Guy L., *More Stewardship Stories*. Harper Bros., New York, 1941.

Morro, William Charles, *Stewardship*. The Bethany Press, St. Louis, 1932.

Mott, John R., *Five Decades and a Forward View*. Harper and Bros., New York, 1939.

Murry, Andrew, *Money; Thoughts for God's Stewards*. Fleming H. Revell, New York, 1897.

Myers, Cortland, *Money Mad*. Fleming H. Revell Co., New York, 1917.

Myers, Harry S. and Agar, F. A., *Workers Together*. Fleming H. Revell, New York, n.d.

Paulson, Irwin G., *It Is To Share*. The Methodist Book Concern, New York, 1931.

Prize Essays, *Gold and The Gospel*. Carlton and Phillips, New York, 1885.

Robinson, A. T., *Tithing for Juniors*. Fleming H. Revell Company, New York, 1930.

Ramsay, Wm., *Church Debts*. Robert E. Peterson, Philadelphia, 1851.

Religious Bodies, Vols. I and II. United States Department of Commerce, Washington, 1930.

Rigell, William R., *Investments in Christian Living*. The Sunday School Board of the Southern Baptist Convention, Nashville, 1930.

Robinson, Emma A., *Stewardship Stories*. Joint Centenary Committee of the Methodist Episcopal Church and the Methodist Episcopal Church, South, New York, 1918.

Sayler, James L., *American Tithers*. The Methodist Book Concern, New York, 1918.

Simpson, John E., *Faithful Also in Much*. Fleming H. Revell, New York, 1932.

———, *This Grace Also*. Fleming H. Revell, New York, 1933.

———, *He That Giveth*. Fleming H. Revell, New York, 1935.

Simpson, John E., *Into My Storehouse.* Fleming H. Revell, New York, 1940.

——, and McKnight, W. J. H., *A Lad's Lunch.* The Layman Foundation, Chicago, n.d.

Stewart, E. B., *The Tithe.* The Winona Publishing Co., Chicago, 1903.

Speer, William, *God's Rule for Christian Giving.* The Presbyterian Board of Publication, Philadelphia, 1875.

Strang, D. W. P., *Studies in Christian Stewardship.* The International Association for Church Finance and Organization, Glasgow, 1931.

Survey of the Field and Work of the Northern Baptist Convention, final edition. National Committee of Northern Baptist Laymen, New York, May, 1919.

The Annual of the Northern Baptist Convention. Northern Baptist Convention, Volumes for 1919 through 1942, New York.

The Annual of the Southern Baptist Convention. Southern Baptist Convention, years 1881, 1883, 1884, 1886, 1887, 1890, 1894, 1897, 1898, 1899, 1900 and 1903 through 1941, Nashville.

The Living Church Annual. The Protestant Episcopal Church, New York.

The Annual Report of the World Service Commission of the Methodist Episcopal Church. World Service Commission, Chicago, 1939.

The Doctrines and Discipline of the Methodist Church. The Methodist Publishing House, New York, 1940.

Thompson, P. W., *The Whole Tithe.* Marshall Brothers, Ltd., London, n.d.

Versteeg, John M., *Save Money.* The Abingdon Press, New York, 1939.

Williamson, Robert Donald, and Wallace, Helen Kingsbury, *Stewardship in the Life of Youth.* Fleming H. Revell, New York, 1926.

Wilson, Bert, *The Christian and His Money Problems.* George H. Doran Company, New York, 1923.

Winburn, H. L., *A Man and His Money.* The Baptist Book Concern, Louisville, 1915.

II. *Books Published Since World War II.*

Andrews, F. Emerson, *Attitude Toward Giving.* Russel Sage Foundation, New York.

——, *Philanthropic Giving.* Russel Sage Foundation, New York.

Bowen, W. A., *God's Wealth and Ours.* Cannaway Printing Co.

Conrad, Alphin, *The Divine Economy.* Wm. B. Eerdman's Publishing Co., Grand Rapids, 1954.

Conrad, Paul H., *This Way to a Thriving Church.* Abingdon-Cokesbury Press, Nashville.

——, *Partnership with Christ.* Judson Press, Philadelphia.

Cushman, Ralph S., *The Message of Stewardship,* Revised Edition. Abingdon-Cokesbury Press, 1946.

Dexter, Harriet Harmon, *Financing Faith.* Bethany Press, St. Louis, 1951.

Dillard, J. E., *Bible Stewardship.* Broadman Press, Nashville.

——, *Good Stewards.* Broadman Press, Nashville.

Ellis, H. W., *Christian Stewardship and Church Finance.* Zondervan Publishing House, Grand Rapids, 1953.

Grace, Frank, *The Concept of Property in Modern Christian Thought.* University of Illinois Press, Urbana.

Grindstaff, W. E., *Developing a Giving Church.* Fleming H. Revell Company, New York, 1954.

Fletcher, Joseph P., *Christianity and Property.* Westminster Press, Philadelphia.

Harrell, Costen J., *Stewardship and the Tithe.* Abingdon-Cokesbury Press, Nashville.

Harrison, Norman B., *Possessing.* The Harrison Service, Minneapolis.

———, *Belonging.* The Harrison Service, Minnapolis.

Hatch, C. W., *Stewardship Enriches Life.* Warner Press, Anderson, Ind.

Herrmann, J. E., *The Chief Steward.* Concordia Publishing House, St. Louis.

Hobbs, Herschel H., *The Gospel of Giving.* Broadman Press, Nashville.

Jenkins, Edmund C., *Philanthropy in America.* Association Press, New York.

Jones, *What Are You Worth.* Bethany Press, St. Louis, 1954.

King, Julius, *Successful Fund Raising Sermons.* Funk and Wagnalls, New York, 1953.

Lansdell, Henry, *The Sacred Tenth.* Baker Book House, Grand Rapids, 1954.

Lindeman, Paul, *My God and I.* Concordia Publishing House, St. Louis.

Lorimor, Albert W., *God Runs My Business.* Fleming H. Revell Company, New York.

Long, Roswell C., *More Stewardship Parables.* Abingdon-Cokesbury Press, Nashville, 1947.

Marts, A. C., *Philanthropy's Role in Civilization.* Harper Brothers, New York.

Miller, Basil, *Treasury of Stewardship Illustrations.* Warner Press, Anderson.

Moore, Merrill D., *Found Faithful.* Broadman Press, Nashville.

Muelder, Walter G., *Religion and Economic Responsibility.* Scribners, New York.

Muncy, W. L., *Fellowship with God through Christian Stewardship.* Central Seminary Press, Kansas City, 1949.

Muncy, W. C., *Trustees of Creation.* Central Seminary Press, Kansas City.

Peterson, Orval, *Stewardship in the Bible.* Bethany Press, St. Louis.

Pierce, Earle V., *The Supreme Beatitude.* Fleming H. Revell Company, New York, 1947.

Rice, John R., *All about Christian Giving.* Sword of the Lord Publishers, Wheaton, 1953.

Robok, D. E., *God and I Are Partners.* Review and Herald Publishing Company.

Rolston, Holmes, *Stewardship in the New Testament.* John Knox Press, Richmond.

Sharp, C. J., *Studies in Christian Stewardship*. The Standard Publishing Company, Cincinnati.

Salstrand, George A. E., *The Tithe, The Minimum Standard of Christian Giving*. Baker Book House, Grand Rapids, 1952.

Shoemaker, Samuel, M., *The Church Alive*. E. P. Dutton and Company, New York.

Siemans, Peter, *The New Testament Conception of Stewardship*. Unpublished Thesis, Northern Baptist Theological Seminary, Chicago, 1952.

Simpson, J. E., *Great Stewards of the Bible*. Fleming H. Revell Company, New York.

Snider, P. M., *The Christian Farmer Works with God*. General Board of Lay Activities of the Methodist Church, Chicago.

Stidger, William, *Human Interest Shares in Christian Stewardship*. General Board of Lay Activities of the Methodist Church, Chicago.

Stoughton, Clarence C., *Whatever You Do*. Muhlenberg Press, Allentown.

Terry, Elizabeth Evans, *Partners with God*. Broadman Press, Nashville.

Thomas, G. Ernest, *Spiritual Life through Tithing*. Tidings Press, Nashville.

———, *To Whom Much Is Given*, Abingdon-Cokesbury Press, Nashville.

Trueblood, Elton, *The Common Ventures of Life*. Harper and Brothers Publishers, New York.

Van Ness, Bethan, F., *The Talking Penny*. Broadman Press, Nashville.

Wolf, Earl C., *My Gold and God*. Beacon Hill Press, Boston, 1947.

III. *Tracts, Pamphlets and Letters.*

Space forbids the publication of the authors, titles and publishers of the some six hundred tracts and pamphlets gathered in this study, also the almost one hundred letters received from stewardship officials and others who were helpful in this study both in 1943 and 1954.

B. Secondary Works

I. *Books*

Calkins, Harvey Reeves, *A Man and His Money*. The Methodist Book Concern, New York, 1914.

Clark, Joseph S., *A Historical Sketch of the Congregational Churches in Massachusetts from* 1620 *to* 1858. Congregational Board of Publication, Boston, 1858.

Lansdell, Henry, *The Sacred Tenth,* Vols. I and II. Society for Promoting Christian Knowledge, London, 1906.

Klett, Guy Soulliard, *Presbyterians in Colonial Pennsylvania*. University of Pennsylvania Press, Philadelphia, 1937.

Sweet, William Warren, *The Story of Religion in America*. Harper and Brothers, New York, 1939.

———, *Religion in Colonial America*. Charles Scribners, New York, 1942.

Vail, A. L., *Stewardship among Baptists*. American Baptist Publication Society, Philadelphia, 1913.

Vedder, Henry C., *A Short History of the Baptists.* American Baptist Publication Society, Philadelphia, n.d.

Weber, H. C., *Evangelism: A Graphic Survey.* The Macmillan Co., New York, 1929.

Weber, H. C., *Presbyterian Statistics through One Hundred Years.* Presbyterian Board of Education, Philadelphia, 1927.

———, *The Horizons of Stewardship.* Fleming H. Revell Company, New York, 1938.

Webster, Richard, *A History of the Presbyterian Church in America from Its Origin to 1760 with Biographical Sketches of Its Early Ministers.* Joseph M. Wilson, Philadelphia, 1857.

Wright, G. Frederich, *Charles Grandison Finney.* The Riverside Press, Cambridge, 1891.

II. *Encyclopedia Articles*

"Pharcellus Church" and "Horace Bushnell" in *Dictionary of American Biography.* Charles Scribner's Sons, New York, 1943.

"Ralph S. Cushman" in *Who's Who In America, 1940-1941, Vol.* 21. The A. N. Marquis Company, Chicago, 1940.

APPENDICES

Explanation of Storehouse Tithers' Association Covenant

Art. I. The important thing in tithing is that the tithe be taken out of the income before any part of it (the income) is used for one's own purposes. In organizing a tithers' association a definite date should be determined on which all members begin to tithe. It should be emphasized that the tithe can be used only for God's work.

Art. II. The association procures cartons of envelopes with one for each Sunday in the year. Envelopes are to have one pocket only and are to be numbered, so that each tither has a number. If the tither has had any income during the week he puts the tithe of it into his envelope for the next Sunday and deposits it on the collection plate to be placed on God's altar with the contribution of those who are not tithers.

Art. III. In organizing, a president, a secretary, and a treasurer, is elected, who, together with the pastor, constitute the executive committee of the association. At the first meeting, and thereafter at the annual meeting, the executive committee recommends that the tithe money shall be divided, so many per cent to the local congregation, so many per cent to the Synod, and the balance to be held as a contingent fund. After the association has adopted the percentages all money is divided accordingly. When the church councilmen take the collection from the altar they separate all the tithing envelopes which should be of a distinctive color and hand them to the treasurer of the S.T.A. The treasurer makes entry on his books by number only. A discreet man should be chosen treasurer. After totaling the receipts for the week the treasurer draws a check payable to the congregation's current expense treasurer for the percentage voted for that purpose. He draws a check payable to the congregation's benevolence treasurer for the percentage voted for Synod. This is then forwarded with the rest of the congregation's benevolence money to the treasurer of Synod. The balance in the treasury which constitutes the contingent fund is available whenever a special appeal is made. It is drawn upon only after vote of the association upon the recommendation of the executive committee. At the close of the year the balance in the contingent fund if any, is paid out by order of the association so that each new year may be begun with an empty treasury. An unused tithe fund is a misplaced trust fund.

Art. IV. Regularity, that is, united action in dispensing the tithe should be encouraged. The presumption is that the association as a whole is better able to determine how the tithe shall be spent to the best advantage, than is the individual.

Art. V. Tithers are not called on during the annual every member canvass. By paying the tithe they are all through. A pledge or dues to a congregational organization must be taken out of the member's tithe and deducted from the percentage of it that goes to the congregation. A pledge to the Seminary or any other Synodical work must be taken out of the member's tithe and deducted from the percentage of it that goes to Synod.

A careful record should be kept by the treasurer, who, if possible, should have some knowledge of accounting. In determining the percentages to congregation and Synod, 40% is recommended for the congregation, and 40% for the Synod, leaving 20% for the contingent fund which is available as in the judgment of the association may seem right and proper, either for local or general work of the church.

APPENDIX II

The Rules and By-Laws of the Storehouse Tithers' Association of the English Lutheran Church, Lacrosse, Wisconsin.

OFFICERS

ARTICLE I.

Section 1. The officers of this Association shall be a President, Secretary, and Treasurer. These together with the Pastor shall constitute the Executive Committee.

DUTIES

ARTICLE II.

Section 1. The duties of the President shall be to preside at all meetings. To appoint all committees. To have general supervision of the affairs of the Association. And to perform all other duties pertinent to his office.

Section 2. The duties of the Secretary shall be to keep precise minutes of all meetings, and after their approval enter them in a book provided for that purpose. To notify members of all special meetings. To carry on the correspondence of the Association. And to perform all other duties pertinent to the office.

Section 3. The duties of the Treasurer shall be to receive all tithe monies from the Church councilmen after service, and from individuals at any time. He shall allot numbers to the members of this Association and shall make entries in his books by numbers only. He shall total the receipts each week and make out a check payable to the congregation's treasurer for the percentage voted for that purpose. He shall draw a check each month payable to the congregation's benevolence treasurer for the percentage voted to synod. He shall execute no orders except those authorized by the Executive Committee. He shall report by totals only the receipts and disbursements at each monthly meeting and at the annual congregational meeting.

EXECUTIVE COMMITTEE

ARTICLE III.

Section 1. The Executive Committee shall have power to act upon the resignation of any of the members. It shall hear all complaints and adjust all difficulties for the welfare of the majority.

Section 2. At the first meeting, and thereafter at the annual meeting, the Executive Committee shall recommend how the tithe money shall be divided. A certain percentage to the local Church, a certain percentage to the work of synod, and the balance held as a contingent fund.

Section 3. The contingent fund may be drawn on for any special appeal upon recommendation of the Executive Committee and a vote of the Association.

MEMBERSHIP

ARTICLE IV.

Section 1. The membership in this organization shall be active and associate.

Section 2. All members of this Association, who tithe, and who have signed and subscribed to the Storehouse Tithers' Covenant, shall be considered active members.

Section 3. All members whose parents are active members and who have no individual income may become associate members of this Association.

VOTING AND ELECTION

ARTICLE V.

Section 1. Only active members of this Association shall be entitled to vote.

Section 2. No minor, whether active or not, shall be permitted to hold office.

Section 3. All voting shall be done by ballot and a majority shall constitute an election.

MONIES

ARTICLE VI.

Section 1. All monies received each Sunday shall be proportioned in accordance with the vote of the majority of the members of this Association. A certain percentage to local work, a certain percentage to synod, and a certain percentage to remain in a contingent fund.

Section 2. The contingent fund shall be available for all special appeals for local or general work of the Church as the members may decide.

Section 3. At the close of the year the balance in the contingent fund, if any, shall be paid out by order of the Association, upon recommendation of the Executive Committee, so that each year may be begun with an empty treasury.

MEETINGS

ARTICLE VII.

Section 1. The regular meeting of the Storehouse Tithers' Association shall be held on the second Sunday of each month, at the time and place designated by the Executive Committee.

Section 2. The regular January meeting shall be held each year on the Sunday following the regular annual congregational meeting and shall constitute the annual meeting of this Association. The fiscal year shall be from January first to December thirty-first.

Section 3. Special meetings may be called by the Pastor, the President, or any three members of the Association.

Section 4. A majority of the members shall constitute a quorum.

AMENDMENTS

ARTICLE VIII.

Section 1. These By-laws may be appended or amended at the annual meeting, provided notice be made in writing, stating the proposed additions or changes at least two weeks prior to the meeting.

INDEX

168 *The Story of Stewardship*